Henry J Kintz

The Inauguration of Grover Cleveland, the President-Elect. March 4th, 1885

A book for fifty million people

Henry J Kintz

The Inauguration of Grover Cleveland, the President-Elect. March 4th, 1885
A book for fifty million people

ISBN/EAN: 9783337402631

Printed in Europe, USA, Canada, Australia, Japan

Cover: Foto ©Suzi / pixelio.de

More available books at **www.hansebooks.com**

THE

INAUGURATION

OF

GROVER CLEVELAND,

THE PRESIDENT-ELECT.

MARCH 4TH, 1885.

A BOOK FOR FIFTY MILLION PEOPLE.

BY

HENRY J. KINTZ.

ALEXANDRIA, VA.
1885.

Wm. F. Fell & Co.,
ELECTROTYPERS AND PRINTERS,
1220–24 SANSOM STREET,
PHILADELPHIA.

HENRY HUDSON. FERDINAND DE SOTO.

LORD BALTIMORE. W^{M.} PENN. BENJAMIN FRANKLIN.

PATRICK HENRY. ALEXANDER HAMILTON.

CONTENTS.

vi   *Contents.*

INTRODUCTION.

In the production of this book, I have endeavored to impress on the minds of my readers the great importance of our Nation's welfare, and that of its subjects; also to set forth some strong facts showing that it is the duty of every American citizen to seek to elevate his fellow-man, without regard to section, creed or politics. Should I succeed in this, my object is attained.

H. J. KINTZ.

Biographical Sketches.

GROVER CLEVELAND,

The President-elect, is a native of the State of New Jersey, and is forty-six years of age. He is a strongly built man, thick set, and the picture of health. His home is in the city of Buffalo, Erie County, New York.

He is of good parentage, and as a boy was noted for his integrity and honesty, and for his quiet and unassuming manners. When a young man, he spent a considerable portion of his time at Theresa, N. Y., with his sister, Mrs. Hoyt, and all who were acquainted with him there still respect him, for his good and sterling qualities. He was elected Governor of the State of New

11

York in the Fall of 1882, by a majority of nearly 200,000 votes.

He is regarded by all who know him as a strict business man, and considering himself an officer of the people, and not a representative only of the party who elected him, he has always performed his official duties to the best of his ability. It is said that when he was Mayor of the City of Buffalo a party favor was asked of him, which he refused, with the remark, that he was sworn in as mayor of the city, for all its people, and not for any particular party. Consequently, he must consider an official oath of a higher and greater importance than the patronage of any politician or lobbyist. In the whole of his career as a public officer, he has made many friends by his straightforward dealings in all that pertained to the welfare of his constituents. Therefore, we may expect that he will make a careful survey of the whole political field before moving in any one direction, and in the selection of his Cabinet will choose such men as he knows to be statesmen, and true to their country and party. Any one who has been unfaithful to the cause of liberty, and not respected the old flag, had better pause to reflect before asking too much of the next President. We have every reason to believe that in his messages to Congress he will advise measures for the promotion of our welfare and happiness, and for the interests of this country, regardless of party or platform, or old fogy principles. We may look forward to having a live Democrat of the times to minister to our wants and those of the nation, instead of one who is twenty-four years behind them. It is not very likely that he will impede the progress of the march of improvement inaugurated by the Republican party, but, on the contrary, advance its cause by letting the ball roll on, and complete what has been left undone by the past Administration.

If so, All Hail to the Chief.

THOMAS HENDRICKS is a native of Pennsylvania, but removed from there to Ohio, and thence to Indiana, where he now resides,

in Indianapolis.   He is over sixty-five years
old, and has been a politician ever since
his first vote.   He was associated on the
ticket with Samuel J. Tilden when he ran
for President, in 1876.   He is a very able
man, and is noted for his social qualities.
He has ever been an old-school Democrat; therefore he will have to knock the
scales off his eyes and march to the front,
if he wishes to be a help to the incoming
administration and to national advance-
ment.

THE STATES

That Have Produced the Men for Presidents.

———

Illinois .... { Abraham Lincoln,
Ulysses S. Grant.

Louisiana....................... Zachary Taylor.

Massachusetts.................. { John Adams,
John Quincy Adams.

New York..................... {
Martin Van Buren,
Millard Fillmore,
Chester A. Arthur,
and President-elect
Grover Cleveland.

New Hampshire............... Franklin Pierce.

Ohio........................... {
Henry Harrison,
Rutherford B. Hayes,
James A. Garfield.

Pennsylvania.................. James Buchanan.

Tennessee...................... {
Andrew Jackson,
James K. Polk,
Andrew Johnson.

Virginia .... {
George Washington,
Thomas Jefferson,
James Madison,
James Monroe,
John Tyler.

15

OFFICIAL CANVASS.

States.	Blaine. Rep.	Cleveland. Dem.	Butler. Peo.	St. John. Pro.	Scattering.
Alabama . . .	59,444	92,973	762	610	10
Arkansas . .	50,895	72,927	1847	. . . .	. .
California . .	102,397	89,264	2017	2920	. .
Colorado . . .	36,277	27,627	1957	759	. .
Connecticut . .	65,898	67,182	1685	2494	. .
Delaware . .	12,778	17,054	6	55	. .
Florida . . .	28,031	31,769	. . .	74	. .
Georgia . . .	47,603	94,567	125	184	. .
Illinois . . .	350,497	312,314	10,910	12,074	. .
Indiana . . .	238,480	244,992	8293	3018	. .
Iowa	197,082	177,286	. . .	1472	. .
Kansas . . .	154,406	90,132	16,346	4495	. .
Kentucky . .	118,674	102,757	1655	3106	. .
Louisiana . .	46,347	62,546	120	338	. .
Maine . . .	72,209	52,140	3953	2160	. .
Maryland . .	85,699	96,932	531	2794	. .
Massachusetts .	146,724	122,481	24,433	10,026	15
Michigan . .	192,669	189,361	763	18,403	22
Minnesota . .	111,685	70,065	3583	4684	. .
Mississippi . .	42,774	78,547	. . . .	. .	. .
Missouri . .	202,029	235,988	. . .	2153	. .
Nebraska . .	76,877	54,354	. . .	2858	. .
Nevada . . .	7,193	5,577	. . . .	. .	. .
New Hampshire	43,249	39,192	552	1575	. .
New Jersey . .	123,436	127,798	3496	6159	. .
New York . .	562,005	563,154	17,064	25,003	709
North Carolina .	125,068	142,905	. . .	448	. .
Ohio	400,082	368,280	5179	11,069	. '
Oregon . . .	26,852	24,593	723	488	. .
Pennsylvania .	474,268	393,747	16,992	15,306	. .
Rhode Island .	19,030	12,394	422	928	1237
South Carolina .	21,733	69,890	. . . .	. .	. .
Tennessee . .	124,078	133,258	957	1131	. .
Texas	88,353	223,208	3321	3511	. .
Vermont . . .	38,411	17.342	785	1612	. .
Virginia . . .	139,356	145,497	. . .	143	7
West Virginia .	63,913	67,331	805	927	. .
Wisconsin . .	161,157	146,477	4598	7656	. .
Total . . .	4,847,659	4,913,901	133,880	150,633	2000
Plurality . .		66,242			

The whole vote cast November 4, 1884, for President was 10,048,073, of which

Cleveland received . 4,913,659.

Blaine . . . 4,847,659.

St. John . . . 150,634.

Butler . . . 133,880.

Scattering . . . 2,000.

Plurality of the popular vote is 66,242.

GEORGE WASHINGTON

JOHN ADAMS

THOMA

JAMES MADISON

REVIEW

OF

THE PRESIDENTIAL CAMPAIGN OF 1884, AND ITS RESULTS.

The great campaign of 1884, with all its different factions and bitter strife, has ended, and will be handed down, in the annals of our country's history, as one of the most remarkable campaigns of the United States of America.

All previous histories of our nation's politics are unlike the last, when the people elected, by their choice, Grover Cleveland President. Never before was the number of aspirants so large; four men and one woman ran, on their respective tickets, for President, and, of course, they all knew that only one could be elected. The vote was never so great, nor so closely contested between the two leading candidates, and for

19

fourteen long days did the people await the
result of the official count.

The excitement reached fever heat, and
had it not been for the fact that the American people have confidence in their method
of franchise, the consequence might have
been bloodshed.

But finally, when the glad tidings flashed
across the electric wires that Grover Cleveland was elected President, by the vote of
the State of New York, the clouds dispersed,
the excitement quieted down, people re-
sumed their various vocations, and business
returned to its normal condition.

Where is the nation that could have
passed through such an ordeal and so
much political strife as successfully as our
country has done?

The victorious party, on hearing the tidings, caught up the glad refrain, and then
went up a long and protracted shout of
victory.

Ten thousand voters raised their voices
in unanimous praise and thanksgiving, cry-
ing, "the jubilee has come." Thousands of

bands mingled their joyous strains, and the reverberation from many cannon mouths shook the pedestals of all the statuary in our public parks, as they stood, cold and mute, in the air of that crisp November evening, until, in the light of the pale moon, they seemed to spring to life, and cast a returning smile to that of a great and prosperous people.

Then tell me where is the Nation whose people could have gone through such a campaign, and after such excitement and turmoil, return to their homes and vocations as we have done?

But remember that this is a country of the people, and ruled by the people. Yes, it is true, this is a great Democracy, and in its elections "fair play" must be its motto : so long as every American does his duty as a citizen our country is safe.

After long, weary nights of toil and anxiety, of hopes and of fears, the former rivals laid their heads on the pillow of rest, and took a refreshing slumber. It is to be hoped they have come out of this political contest wiser and better men.

Even Mrs. Belva Lockwood rejoiced in the end of a strife such as had never before fallen to the lot of an American woman, and she congratulated herself on the good fortune of having emerged from it to her advantage.

In the history of American politics this is the first instance to be recorded where a woman and a mother entered into competition for the Presidency of the United States. And now, the precedent being established, no one can tell whether it will end in success or defeat, for small beginnings have, in many instances, proved great enterprises and successes. So let the fair sex never be tired of well doing ; for what would be our country without our wives and sweethearts ? We will look with pleasure on their efforts, and await future developments in this new field of enterprise ; for who knows—we may yet have a vice-president, if not a president, from among their number.

For twenty-four years the Democratic party has been, as it were, out in the cold, trammeled by misfortune and poor management, and marshaled to defeat when victory had almost perched herself on its banner. Its condition is expressed in the language of the forlorn refrain : "so near, and yet so far." During those long twenty-odd years, in one of every four, the Democrats could only witness their opponents enjoy the inauguration of their successful candidate, and were not allowed to enter, so to speak, into the Holy of Holies. But now, after patient endurance in the past, and desperate efforts in the recent campaign, they appear before us as victors, feeling as if the millennium had come. They are on the threshold of a great, coming event—the inauguration of their choice— when they will make one of the grandest displays that has ever been witnessed in the Capital of the American Nation. Nor will it be out of place to say that the Republicans will enjoy it to a considerable

extent, as they claim for one of their
mottoes, " Live and let live."

Then let them rejoice with those who are
happy, and sympathize with those who are
afflicted; which they surely have done in
the past few years. Look at this country's
great fires; its scourges of sickness and
other disasters; relieved by their charity,
their bountiful provisions and timely succor.

Twenty-four years is a long time to wait;
but like the promise made to Jacob, of old,
the prize is gained at last.

But we must remember that the Democratic party is composed of men who have
not been idle through these long years.
No, not by any means; but, on the contrary,
they have been strictly attending to their
own business, and have had the advantages
of a rich country and a live administration.
They have thus accumulated wealth manifold, and have improved their homes, and
carefully guarded the welfare of those dear
to them.

If I am not mistaken, their true happiness
was greater in the past, when out of office,

than it will be in the future, with all power; for the full enjoyment of all privileges is sometimes preferable to the administration of them, especially when there is so much strife and bitter feeling engendered by the effort to gain the right of supremacy.

Let the ball of state roll on; for whoever undertakes to stop it will only be crushed by its progress. Old-time and old-fogy principles are not now adapted for the American people. They are a progressive nation and expect to remain so. Advance is the watchword.

There is no time to pause or endeavor to turn back: the wheels of time make their revolutions, and have done so forever: yesterday has passed for you and for me, dear reader, and it now remains to get ready to live, not to die. I find no proof between the lids of Holy Writ that I must die. Life everlasting is my theme, and shall be henceforth.

" Forever float the standard sheet;
   Where's the foe but falls before us,
With freedom's soil beneath our feet,"
   And life eternal promised to us.

I surely believe that all things work for the best.   And for whom?

For those who love God.

And we claim to be a nation that does love and fear our great Creator.   We have the promise of His protection, and if our nation shall live as it ought, in that fear and love, benefiting its subjects thereby, it need not dread the great change that is spoken of by our Protector, on the last day, when He will display His power and glory.

It has been said that this nation is growing more wicked and corrupt.

Not so.

The false theory that we are getting worse instead of better has been advanced by some, with a view of palliating their own misconceptions and errors; but by a studious observation of their words and actions, I have discovered that these same men, when closely pressed, seem to grope more in the dark than at first.   For instance, Ingersoll, after his many lectures and public utterances, exploded his theory, in the funeral sermon delivered over his brother, when he ended, if I am not mistaken, with these words, or the substance of them : "Wrecked on the shores of time, hoping for the best."

Now, after having been so zealous in endeavoring to convince men of the truth of his views, why should he wreck them at the very moment they need assistance? for we cannot suppose that man is able to pass through such an ordeal alone. Wrecked means ruined, or, at least, to suffer loss. Ingersoll may have used the word, "stranded;" but if he did, the meaning is the same.

Now, my dear reader, what right has any man to destroy your hope, unless he first give you some foundation for a better one. No man is justified in robbing you of your faith, if he cannot supply one more perfect in its stead ; and this has never yet been found.

Then walk steadfastly in the true path, which never fails to lead men to happiness. Sincere worship of God, and pure, unselfish

motives, will guide you safely through
trouble and ruin; and as the great Jehovah
is able to take care of His people, they
are growing better daily: hence, this nation
must surely be advancing in civilization
and Christian fellowship with God.

The large increase of our population, by
its natural resources and immigration, is
adding hundreds of thousands to our num-
bers yearly; and there must be some means
provided to feed, clothe and educate them
to be true American citizens. There is a
duty to be performed in the future, which the
American people have thus far neglected,
and that is, that when foreigners come to our
country they should be made to understand
that this is America, and that to become
citizens they will be required to adopt
American principles, and while they are
enjoying the protection and all the privileges of a free nation, to refrain from instill-
ing into their children's minds the idea that
they are living in Italy, Germany, Ireland,
or any other European country.

American freedom is not constituted on

narrow-minded or prejudiced principles; men and women are not to live here, as it were, in their own shells, without regard to their fellow man. On the contrary, every man should be ready to help elevate his neighbor, as we do not know what time may bring forth, nor how near the ties of family relation may be drawn. In helping one another we may thus be of service to a future son-in-law or daughter-in-law. True American principles do not confine themselves to sectarian strifes nor sectional schools, neither are they bounded by the points of the compass.

What is a benefit to one State will directly or indirectly benefit all; just so with a neighborhood—what is an advantage to one is profitable to all, provided it fosters a true and legitimate business.

This nation, in the last twenty-five years, has grown more in beauty, grandeur and wealth than in the fifty years preceding, and in intelligence, wisdom and science is the equal of any country on the face of the globe. Nor has it been idle in religious

JAMES MONROE.

JOHN QUINCY ADAMS.

ANDREW JACKSON.

MARTIN VAN BUREN.

matters, for to-day we can boast of numerous churches and public institutions of charity.

When we pause to consider all this, we must admit that there is a Supreme Ruler who watches over the destinies of our country, and that He is fully competent to guide the affairs of His kingdom; therefore, I repeat, that at the present time, we are further advanced in every respect than we have ever been before.

There are a great many things yet to be done, and much room for improvement; for as this nation develops itself its wants multiply; but it seems as if Providence had so ordained, that as our demands increase, ingenuity supplies them with different inventions.

It has not been long since a noted lord of England thought it was impossible to engineer a railroad with success, and advanced the idea that if a cow should get on the track, there would be no remedy; but he was told by the inventor that "it would be bad for the cow, my lord." In the history of railroads, it has proved, in many instances, to be bad for both the railroad and the cow. But trains move on, and that, too, on time; old fogyism does not stop them; and now it is only a matter of time and money, to have friends hundreds of miles apart meet each other in a few short hours.

The history of our country has been written by so many different authors, that it is hardly necessary for me even to speak of it here; but I must refer my reader to its pages, in order to convince him that this country's constitution is founded on a different basis from that of monarchies; and when one reflects upon the great and glorious boon of freedom which we enjoy, he cannot refrain from exclaiming, in joy similar to that of the noble Roman :—

"I, too, am an American."

Proud, happy America! How many poor, down-trodden victims of misfortune have found rest and shelter on thy hospitable soil! How many families have been re-deemed from poverty and disgrace, to find homes and honors awaiting them here. England, with its iron-shod heel, crushed many a poor soul to the earth, until the pressure was too galling to bear, and she was compelled to release her struggling victims. Thanks be to God that such a victory can be recorded in the history of America.

The aristocracy of the old world held the poor man under, and would still continue to do so, but for the discovery of America and its glorious results. Men have found out that the freedom of this nation has worked miracles for the human family, and will do so to the end of time. They know, too, that great emperors or kings, presidents or governors do not wear much larger coats than their fellow men, and, in many cases, are far inferior in knowledge to their humbler subjects.

Then let all kings, emperors, presidents and governors beware how they conduct themselves, for ten thousand thousand eyes are constantly on the alert, watching their every action and movement. A veto,

c

ABRAHAM LINCOLN.

JAMES BUCHANAN.

FRANKLIN PIERCE.

ANDREW JOHNSON.

or a sanction of a bill, at this period, is known to all ends of the earth, in a very short time, and is freely discussed by men in all the walks of life. Incidents and events are commented upon in the workshop as well as in the pulpit or at the bar. We have seen, among the great rulers of our country, one, who, from the humble occupation of a' rail splitter, rose to the highest office in the gift of the American people—that of President of the United States. It was he, who, by his unerring judgment alone, saved our beloved country in the hour of her greatest need. Let all heads bow in reverence to the memory of Abraham Lincoln.

The poor boy who ate his bread as he walked the streets of Philadelphia snatched lightning from the heavens and converted it to his own use; and to-day it is the means by which we can converse with friends many miles away, and with our own voices.

Old fogies have called men fools, and, in the course of time, have become convinced who the real fools were, and have

been men enough to acknowledge them
selves in the wrong.

The best families sometimes make mistakes, and only awake to consciousness
when too late to avert the evil consequences of their errors; like the unlucky
huntsman, who, mistaking his target, pulls
the fatal trigger, hears the loud report,
and rushing to secure his game, finds it
has escaped him. It is then he truly
realizes his situation.

Governments, like individuals, can com-
mit grave errors, and they are much more
difficult to correct.

When a faction of the Democratic party
sold its electors to Horace Greeley, it made
a sale, but in that transaction it failed to
deliver all its goods. It is true, many a
good Democratic citizen was delivered,
but there were others, equally as good,
who were not, and the results are known.

But in this campaign a reunion has taken
place, and victory is ours. Now it remains
to be seen what the party will do for the
benefit of our country; for, as we well

know, this is a government for the people, and when the chief magistrate is sworn in, he becomes the president of all the people alike.

In the policy of the next administration, which will be that of Grover Cleveland, three words will be sufficient for guidance, if adhered to properly; these are, "Industry, Progress and Protection." As self preservation is the first law of nature with man, so it must be with a nation. If this country was ever worth fighting for, it is also worth protecting, lest, in the hour when least expected, the foe may appear and bear away the prize.

It is said that when a vulture swoops down upon a flock, it always takes the choicest.

People who need to earn their bread by the sweat of their brow must have employment, and there is enough to do for all, if properly managed; it is much better to keep them in the workshops than in the prisons and almshouses.

I ask any statesman what will be the

COLUMBUS

PONCE DE LEON

SEBASTIAN CABOT

consequence if improvement is stopped, and our mechanics idle, or obliged to compete with the cheap labor of other nations. It would drive them and their families from our churches and schools, simply for want of proper food and clothing.

Nor can this nation afford to have bread riots, caused by a stagnation in business, merely to conform with some old fogy principles. There is no time now to cry for spilt soup which has evaporated years ago. The past has gone forever, and we must look ahead, not back, for the breakers that will destroy the ship are not behind it, but before; so stand to the helm and watch.

Columbus went forth to discover America; he did not seek it in the interior of Spain. Nations, like men, must await their opportunities and improve them.

The time is not far distant when new issues will appear before the people. The conflicts caused by agitators in trade unions have already begun, and those who claim to be mechanics, but too good to

work, are trying to array labor against
capital.   Not the true laboring mechanic,
for he works to earn his bread ; but the
mechanic who has grown beyond his business, and, wishing to secure aggrandise-
ment, presses himself upon the true laboring mechanic to attain his object.   My dear
reader, did you ever contemplate the result
of labor arrayed against capital ?   Why,
sir, it would ruin both these great elements
that are absolutely necessary for the progress of any great nation.   Capital, it is
true, could consume herself and live for
a time; but, on the contrary, labor could
not; and if you withdraw labor from capital, capital suffers, while labor really starves.
The results would immediately lead to
bread riots, war, famine, arson and all
other evils that can be conceived.

Now let our great statesmen remember,
that when a country has attained a population like this—of fifty-five millions of
people—there must be a union of its best
men.   These are the capitalists and laborers,
who, to be prosperous, must walk hand in

hand, and fight, if necessary, to protect each other; for in their mutual confidence lies their power. The capitalist who puts his million in an enterprise, perhaps invests his whole fortune; he may employ a hundred men, who only give their daily labor, and at the end of the week receive their compensation; but the enterprise may be a failure, and he loses his all, while the laborer is disappointed in his job, but the next day is ready to work at another.

In the history of labor strikes, in this country as in others, we find they always prove to be a loss to the striker as well as to all connected with them. Now if this be a fact, which I believe it is, why should this government allow agitators to play their pranks on innocent and unsuspicious people? Take, for example, the history of the Rebellion, which was permitted to grow openly to maturity, under the immediate presence of James Buchanan, the sworn President of the United States. The government should learn from its past experience how to conduct its future policy.

History, it is claimed, repeats itself; if so, let the coming administration and all great political parties take heed, when they see the timbers of a great structure beginning to part, to stand from under, lest it fall and crush them. Nations, kingdoms and parties will recognize, in this comparison, that "united, we stand, divided, we fall," has an important and significant meaning.

The recent fall of the Republican party illustrates the old proverb: "Rule or Ruin." The latter generally ends most disastrously for the leader; and, I would add to this, that good management consists in the ability to direct affairs to the best advantage of those concerned, whether they be a nation or a party.

The past campaign has been a peculiar one; the various issues involved and opinions expressed, together with its different candidates, have brought before the people some new ideas, as well as suggested a few well-merited criticisms.

In the first place, when the Republican party was in convention at Chicago, the

Stalwarts and Half-breeds showed their variance at once, and their ambition, it would seem, was not so much the successful nomination of their candidate, as it was the defeat of the opposing element, no matter how fatal the result might prove to the party. Rule or ruin must have been the motto of the two leading aspirants. Both factions were eager to grasp the prize, but appeared to think only of the present rival, not the outside foe; and while they were providing a way, as they each supposed, to success, they were simply paving the road for their enemy to ride to victory.

In like manner, when the Democrats held their convention in the same room, some time after, a similar feeling prevailed; while the old Democratic leaders made their wants known, the element of true progress in the party was clamoring to have its views on the subject heard and adopted. They claimed that, as the old faction had led them so many times to defeat, their true policy was to shake off the old fogy principles of the party, and, as

it were, reorganize it, by coming to the front
with a live platform ; and they made many
a speech which originated new ideas in
the minds of all who heard them. One,
in particular, was made by a representative
from the East, who referred to the New
York delegation in these terms : "You are
slaves, and talking with the tongues of your
masters." No truer words were ever uttered,
in my opinion, than these; for many a
Democrat has worked under the lash of that
bondage, rather than stand out and be a
free man. They have done so ever since
their first vote was cast; and also at the
very time of the nomination of General
George B. McClellan, when that faction
tied on his neck the placard that the war
was a failure, and demanded immediate
settlement.

It has swayed its sceptre of power with a
bold, fierce hand, and has led the Democratic party to defeat. It would have done
so in the last campaign, had it not been for
the mistakes of those Republican leaders,
who have fallen into the same vice; for

virtually, although their candidate has been
the victorious one, the Democrats received
their greatest defeat in the recent contest—
a defeat equal to that of Grace, who ran
for the office of Mayor of the city of New
York in 1880.

Had the members of the Democratic
party, in convention at Chicago, adhered
to wholesome advice, they would have
carried the greater portion of all the Northern States. With the feeling of the com-
munity, the three words, "Industry, Progress and Protection," would have been
the only platform needed to do so, and,
short as it would have been, every elector
could have understood its meaning.

The race would have been won so easily
that the Democratic horse would have
reached the goal, been taken in and
groomed, before the Republican one could
have been seen in the distance.

But it all happened for the best; and
since the Democrats have come into power,
simply by a back-hand thrust of the Republican party, the situation will be care-

fully studied, before the work of the next administration begins.

It is certainly more advantageous for a country, that its politics should be divided as equally as possible, for, when such is the case, the candidate of each party has greater respect for his constituents.

I must not forget St. John; for he, it is written, was a noted saint, in his day, and a few comments, perhaps, will not disturb his ashes.

The great cause of Temperance no man will discountenance, and Prohibition I will not at present discuss; but in considering the subject of Temperance in all its bearings, I do not feel that I trespass on the rights or interests of any man ; but, on the contrary, think it my duty and privilege to say a few words to my readers on so important a matter.

In the first place, I sincerely believe that God, in His all-wise providence, created man perfect, and in giving him his different desires and passions, made them holy ; or, to be fully understood, I may say, all the passions of men are holy ones. But man is a free moral agent, and can do as he pleases, excepting therefrom, always, that he control his passions and not allow them to control him. The only true way to be temperate is in the practice of this theory; so I believe, at least, and judge I am correct. Nay, further; I believe my readers will sustain me in this assertion.

In the organization of the Prohibition party, the Temperance people did the very best thing that ever was undertaken for that cause; it was high time to marshal together their forces, and no one could have objected to it and make such objection honestly. For, while they were organizing, they had a perfect right to drill their men, and had St. John, as well as others who undertook the generalship, been wise, they would have achieved a brilliant victory. If St. John had marched to the battle-field with his men, and instructed them how to act in order to help their friends wherever they might be found, and then disbanded them, and issued a proclamation that he would not stand between the two great political parties of the country, but only claim protection from the victor, to-day the cause of Temperance would be in the ascendant. No matter how the contest should have been decided, whether for Cleveland or Blaine, the successful candidate would have been in duty bound to recognize him and his adherents. For twenty long years they have struggled to obtain a foothold in the land, only, it would seem, to be led up to the cannon's mouth for their destruction.

On the laboring men's ticket I will not dwell, for it exploded prematurely : nevertheless, I will say, that those who take Benjamin Butler for a fool had better first pull the beam out of their own eye.

I greatly admire the new political field that Mrs. Lockwood and her followers have presented to the gentler sex, and I heartily wish God-speed to their cause, particularly if it be a good one, as I sincerely trust it is. At some future day I hope to see the good women of our country accorded the right of an equal representation.

WM HENRY HARRISON.

JOHN TYLER.

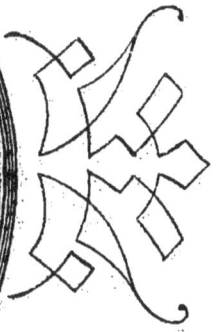

JAMES K. POLK.

MISS COLUMBIA.

Mid all the nations on the globe,
Where shall we go to find a robe
To dress our daughter for the ball,
And crown her fairest of them all?

In years she is not far advanced;
But every young man is entranced
When gazing on her youthful face,
Its wondrous beauty and sweet grace.

'Tis for the great Inauguration
She must be clothed to suit her station;
We could not let it go to press,
That she had not a suitable dress.

Her Uncle Sam has racked his brain,
And speaks of France, and then of Spain;
But silk and lace she must not wear,
Though one is rich, the other rare.

He says that she is his delight,
And must look regal to the sight,
But not like any silly flirt;
So burnished bronze will be her skirt.

Her waist will be of polished steel,
Costly and bright, yet very genteel,
And round it clasped a belt of gold,
Enriched with diamonds manifold.

Necklace and bracelets set with charms,
Will circle her neck and well-formed arms,
While silver will her hose complete,
And finest glass encase her feet.

In golden waves will fall her hair
Around her brow and form so fair,
With jewels peeping in and out,
And dainty blossoms round about.

And now behold you, one and all,
Arrayed and ready for the ball,
She stands, our loved Columbia,
The daughter of America.

Let every man his homage pay
To our sweet queen this festal day,
And wave his cap, and proudly cry,
For her I live, for her will die.

Then let every nation a fair warning take ;
Who dares to offend her retribution must make ;
And after this evening she'll stay quietly home,
Where any may find her, on the Capitol dome.

THE INAUGURATION.

In the inauguration of our different presidents, either party has made more or less demonstration, but on the occasion so near at hand we may expect one of the grandest displays of the kind ever witnessed in Washington. The beautiful paved streets and wide avenues of our Capital make it one of the finest cities in the world for the exhibition of well-drilled companies and civic organizations, while its climate, generally speaking, is pleasant and healthful at that time of the year. Of course, we have had some cold and disagreeable days, but, by comparison, these are few in number.

So we may hope that the 4th of March, 1885, will dawn in unusual light and splendor over the most beautiful city in America. The statue of the Goddess of Liberty will smile in the sun's reflected brightness, and from her shoulders will float the Star-spangled banner; her face will be powdered with the frost of a March morning, and life will be all that is wanting to see her wave her cap in honor of her country.

Uncle Sam will be abroad, arrayed in a suit made from the flag of Bunker Hill, and he will walk along with a quick, proud step, as he always does when such an imposing ceremony is to take place.

His tall beaver will be raised to Miss Columbia, as he passes through the Capitol grounds, and his eager glance will note the many and extensive preparations for the day's festivities. He will go immediately to the White House, to inform Chester A. Arthur that he is expected to vacate at one o'clock precisely, and at the same time bid him escort the president elect to the Capitol, in his private carriage, drawn by six horses, two blacks, two whites, and two bays. He will also inform him that he must fasten in the lappel of Grover Cleveland's coat a Marshal Neil rosebud, taken from the conservatory of the White House, and then introduce him to Chief Justice Waite, who will administer the oath of office.

Having so ordered, Uncle Sam will
walk home with elastic step, and get his
breakfast, which he usually takes at eight
o'clock. By this time the streets will be
in a bustle, from the curbstone to the top of
the Monument, and the city will be alive
with pedestrians and vehicles. Life and
beauty will be the order of the day, and
the happiest people that ever thronged a
capitol will be found in Washington.

There will be hardly less than a million
of people in the District, for many, in all
parts of the United States and Canada,
have already engaged rooms, and even
windows, to look out on the avenue. Eu-
ropeans, too, have made arrangements to
witness the inaugural ceremonies. Every
one will be expected to be on his good
behavior on that day, and appear in his
holiday attire, to do honor to the occasion.
Men with their wives or sweethearts, or
other relations, will be in the city as early
as the dawn. Special trains will be run on
all the railroads, at reduced rates, to accommodate the many passengers, and steam-

boats from Norfolk and other southern
points will arrive, crowded to their utmost
capacity.

Flora McFlimsy will, in all probability,
make her presence known at this time, as
we can safely suppose, she has at last found
something to wear. It is said that at the
last inauguration, that of Garfield, after
looking over her wardrobe of one hundred and one different dresses, she sat
down and cried, because she could find
nothing suitable to wear. However, Uncle
Sam paid her a visit since, and offered her
the flag of Barbara Fritchee, which she
declined, with the remark that its texture
was too old, but to please him she would
immediately order a handsome dress from
Paris, made by Worth. If these rumors
are correct, we may expect her, knowing
that she will be welcomed with hearty
cheers, as it has been a long time since
her last appearance in society.

All the belles of Washington will be
out, and with them their lady cousins from
Baltimore, whom they have invited to come

and enjoy the celebration. When these sister cities are represented by the fair sex, I will challenge all the others in the Union to compete with them, for the prize of beauty. This will consist of a very valuable diamond necklace, studded with sapphires, set diagonally, and beautiful in the extreme. It will be presented by a young gentleman from New York, provided he shall see fit to do so, and the young lady accepts his hand.

There will be a representation of the different cities of the South and West, by ladies, and should the weather prove unpropitious, and the streets moist or muddy, there will be a great demand for trailbearers, which can be readily supplied in Washington.

The utmost pains will be taken to have the visitors enjoy themselves, and in all the vacant places along the avenue seats will be erected for the accommodation of the weary, where they can receive rest and comfort for a slight compensation. These seats will be 20,000 or upward, in number,

each competent to hold from two to six
persons, and they will be inspected by
the Building Committee, to insure safety
from accident.

The Inauguration ceremonies will be su-
perintended by a committee of fifty persons,
and Colonel James G. Berret, of Washington, D. C., will act as chairman of said
committee. This has been done by re-
quest of the National Executive Committee,
Dec. 10th, 1884, which is composed of the
following officers :—

HON. A. P. GORMAN, *Chairman.*

Hon. A. H. Garland,	Hon. D. R. Paige,
Hon. John E. Kenna,	Hon. Wm. S. Rosecrans,
Hon. S. M Stockslager,	Hon. J. H. Murphy.
Hon. R. S Stevens,	

HON. GEO. A. POST, *Secretary.*

WATSON BOYLE, *Assistant Secretary.*

A. A. WILSON, *Treasurer.*

The details of the Inauguration ceremonies will be carried out under the supervision of the following Committees :—

GENERAL COMMITTEE.

Col. Berret, Chairman,	Lawrence Gardner,
James E. Harvey, Secretary,	W. D. Davidge,
A. A. Wilson,	M. F. Norris,
John E. Norris,	Major Lydecker,
Dr. Toner,	C. M. Matthews,

RUTHERFORD B. HAYES.

ULYSSES S. GRANT.

JAMES A. GARFIELD.

F. L. Moore,
F. B. McGuire,
J. P. Willett,
C. C. Glover,
F. A. Richardson,
Frank Hume,
G. W. Adams,
H. A. Willard,
Admiral Worden,
W. M. Galt,

R. O. Holtzman,
Gen. McKeever,
Geo. W. Cochran,
Geo. McHenry,
T. J. Luttrell,
Stilson Hutchins,
Gen. J. G. Parke,
Rear Admiral Rodgers,
Thomas J. Fisher.

SUB-COMMITTEES.

I. RECEPTION COMMITTEE,

To take charge of all distinguished guests, especially at the Inauguration Ball.

The Chief Justice and Associate Justices of the Supreme Court of the United States, the Chief Justice and Judges of the Court of Claims, the Chief Justice and Judges of the Supreme Court of the District of Columbia, and the Commissioners of the District of Columbia.

Hon. W. W. Corcoran,
Gen. Richard C. Drum,
Rr. Adm. T. A. Jenkins,
Com. W. W. Queen,
Rr. Adm. C. W. Wells,
Rr. Adm. T. H. Stevens,
Col. Thos. L. Casey,
Hon. G. S. Boutwell,
W D. Davidge,
Hon. Horatio King,
Dr. Daniel P. Clarke,
Geo. A. McIlhenny,
Maj. Frank E. Taylor,
Gen. M. C. Meigs,
Gen. C. McKeever,
John M. Sims,
Col. C. G. McCawley,
Prof. Spencer F. Baird,
Jas. C. Welling, LL D.,
Chas. M. Matthews,
Com. S. B. Franklin,
Paymaster Kenney,
Hon. J. H. McKenney,
Hamilton-G. Fant,
Jas. C. McGuire,
Col. C. J. Bonaparte,
Dr. W. W. Johnston,
Hon. Eppa Hunton,
John A. Baker,
Gen. A. St. Clair Denver,
Dr. C. P. Culver,
Hon. Wash. McLean,

Col. C. Alexander,
Henry S. Davis,
Com. G. C. Remey,
Com. H. F. Picking,
H. O. Claughton,
Linden Kent,
James E. Harvey,
John J. Beall,
Gen. Wm. McKee Dunn,
R. S. Davis,
Col. Wright Rives,
Gen. R. Macfeeley,
Gen. N. L. Anderson,
John Selden,
J. H. McH. Hollingsworth,
R. K. Elliott,
Edward Clarke,
Bennet H. Hill,
E. E. White,
Nathaniel Wilson,
Theodore Sheckels,
William King, Sr.,
W. W. Burdette,
F. C. Dean,
Charles Worthington,
Maj. G. C. Goodloe,
R. Ross Perry,
G. E. Hamilton,
Col. James G. Payne,
G. W. Phillips,
Michael Talty,
John W. Drew,

B. P. Snyder,
Anthony Pollock,
A. H. Lowery,
Surg. Gen. R. Murray,
Dr. G. Maulshy, U. S. N.,
Com. H. C. Taylor,
Gen. P. H. Sheridan,
Hon. George Bancroft,
Maj. Gen. H G. Wright,
Surg. Gen. F. M. Gunnell,
Gen. W B. Hazen,
Comd'r A. A. Semmes,
Comd'r H. L. Howison,
Vice Adm. S. C. Rowan,
John E. Norris,
Rr. Adm. C. R. P. Rodgers,
Maj. G. L. Lydecker,
John W. Thompson,
Hon. R. T. Merrick,
Gen. John G. Parke,
Rob't J. Ingersoll,
Geo. W. Cochran,
F. L. Moore,
Dr. Jos. M. Toner,
Dr. R. S. L. Walsh,
Adm. D. D. Porter,
Comd'r A. H. McCormick,
Comd'r R. D. Evans,
M. W. Galt,
Josiah Dent,
Ben. Perley Poore,
Hon. Jos. H. Bradley,
Dr. A. Y. P. Garnett,
Allen McLane,
A. Ross Ray,
Jeff. Chandler,
Anthony Hyde,
C. W. Bennett,

Mahlon Ashford,
Leigh Robinson,
Titian J. Coffey,
Col. Lorenzo Sigraves,
E. D. Hartley,
Robert W. McHenry,
Wm. H. Tenney,
J. C. G. Kennedy,
Thomas Hyde,
Alex. Porter Morse,
D. R. McKee,
M. W. Beveridge,
Judge T. W. Bartley,
W. B. Webb,
W. F. Mattingly,
W. E. Howard,
John T. Given,
W. R. Riley,
Robert Beall,
John T. Lenman,
S. H. Kauffman,
B. L. Blackford,
Simon Wolf,
William Laird,
Gen. D. Walker,
Mills Dean,
Reginald Fendall,
Benjamin G. Lovejoy,
Henry Polkinhorn,
W. M. Shuster, Sr.,
J. Hollins McBlair,
G. W. Shutt,
B. Robinson,
Dr. N. S. Lincoln,
S. P. Quackenbush,
Maj. Gen. John Newton,
Gen. S. V. Benet.

A Senator and Representative from each State and Territory, as follows:—

Maine—William P. Frye, Nelson Dingley.
New Hampshire—H. W. Blair, J. W. Stewart.
Vermont—George F. Edmunds, Ossian Ray.
Rhode Island—N. W. Aldrich, Jonathan Chace.
Massachusetts—Henry L. Dawes, Patrick A. Collins.
Connecticut—Joseph R. Hawley, William W. Eaton.
New York—E. G. Lapham, Samuel S. Cox.
New Jersey—John R. McPherson, William McAdoo.
Pennsylvania—J. Donald Cameron, Samuel J. Randall.
Delaware—Thomas F. Bayard, Charles B. Lore.
Maryland—James B. Groome, John V. L. Findlay.
Virginia—Henry H. Riddleberger, John S. Barbour.
West Virginia—Johnson N. Camden. C. Philip Snyder.
North Carolina—Zebulon Vance, William R. Cox.
South Carolina—Wade Hampton, Samuel Dibble.
Georgia—Joseph E. Brown, James H. Blount.

Alabama—John T. Morgan, William H. Forney.
Mississippi—L. Q. C. Lamar, O. R. Singleton.
Florida—Charles W. Jones, R. H. M. Davidson.
Louisiania—Benjamin F. Jones, Floyd King.
Texas—Samuel B. Maxey, John H. Reagan.
Ohio—George H. Pendleton, Benjamin Le Fevre.
Michigan—Omar D. Conger, William C. Maybury.
Wisconsin—Angus Cameron, P. V. Deuster.
Indiana—D. W. Voorhees, William S. Holman.
Illinois—John A. Logan, William R. Morrison.
Minnesota—S. J. R. McMillan, Horace B. Strait.
Iowa—William B. Allison, J. H. Murphy.
Missouri—Francis M. Cockrell, A. H. Buckner.
Arkansas—Augustus H Garland, J. K. Jones.
Nebraska—Charles H. Van Wyck, E. K. Valentine.
Nevada—James G. Fair, George W. Cassidy.
Colorado—Nathaniel P. Hill, James P. Belford.
Oregon—James H. Slater, M. C. George.
California—John T. Farley, William S. Rosecrans.
Kentucky—James B. Beck, John G. Carlisle.
Tennessee—Isham G. Harris, George G. Dibrell.
Arizona—G. H. Oury.
Idaho—T. F. Singiser.
Montana—Martin Maginnis.
New Mexico—F. A. Manzanares.
Dakota—J. B. Raymond.
Wyoming—M. E. Post.
Washington—T. H. Brents.
Utah—J. T. Caine.

2. FINANCE COMMITTEE,

To receive funds and to turn them over to the treasurer, whose
office, this committee respectfully suggest, should be created

Levi Z. Leiter, Chairman,
W. W. Corcoran,
D. Willis James,
Alexander Mitchell,
Eugene Kelley,
W. C. Whitney,
E. R. Bacon,
R. T. Woodward,
Erastus Corning,
John R. McLean,
George W. Childs,
Gardner G. Hubbard,
Eckley B. Cone,
Addison Cammack,
Edward Cooper,
Hugh J. Grant,
Charles B. Button,
William R. Travers,
Gen. John B. Gordon,
Thomas M. Lanahan,
H. Grafton Dulaney,
John Arnot,
B. S. Stevens,
Hon. Leopold Morse,
M. W. Galt,
Daniel B. Clarke,
H. M. Sweeney,
John W. Thompson,
M. G. Emery,
Edward Weston,
Gen. N. L. Anderson,
John E. Kendall,
Norris Peters,
Charles Payson,
Joseph C. McKibbin,
D. W. Mahon,
P. H. Hooe,
Hon. R. P. Flower,
Robert Garrett,
Joseph J. O'Donohue,
William L. Scott,
O. H. Payne,
August Belmont,
Maj. W. H. Thomas,
Jonathan Scoville,
Charles J. Canda,
A. J. Drexel,
B. K. Jamison,

John Cadwallader, Jr.,
B. J. McGrann,
A. S. Hewitt,
William R. Grace,
O. B. Potter,
George H. B. White,
Jesse Seligman, Jr.,
Hon. Henry G. Davis,
Robert Beverly,
Isaac Bell, Jr.,
Charles L. Mitchell,
F. O. Prince,
James Sloan, Jr.,
Edward Temple,
E. Frank Riggs,
Samuel Norment,
John A. J. Creswell,

Lewis G. Davis,
C. J. Hillyer,
Jesse B. Wilson,
Henry A. Willard,
James S. Edwards,
Charles J. Bell,
R. O. Holtzman,
S. T. Suit,
William E. Clarke, Alexandria, Va.
G. G. Young, Brooklyn, N. Y.
David King, Newport, R. I.
James J. Faye, New York.
S. T. House, Helena, Mont.
James E. Coleman, San Francisco.
Theodore W. Myers, New York.
E. Kurtz Johnson, Colorado.

3. COMMITTEE ON PUBLIC COMFORT,

To procure and furnish information in reference to the accommodation of visitors.

L. Gardner, Chairman,
Thos. E. Waggaman,
H. O. Towles,
C. C. Willard,
C. W. Spofford,
Frank Hollingshead,
Charles S. Moore,
Thomas H. Harbin,
John L. Voght,
Gen. Geo. W. Dyer,
Isaac Landic,
W. S. Thompson,
W. W. Kirby,
P. J. Duffy,
E. F. Buckley,
John S. Miller,
O. G. Staples,
James Lansburgh,
I. Saks,
John B. Scott,
M. G. McCormick,
A. H. Stephenson,
J. Brad. Adams,
Henry Hurt,
W. R. Brown,
Dr. C. M. Hammett,
James Bagan,
J. W. Kennedy,
A. W. Fletcher,
Geo. E. Kennedy,
John D. Bartlett,
Dr. A. P. Fardon,
B. H. Stinemetz,
Dr. H. I. Murray,
Dr. G. P. Fenwick,

E. J. Burtt,
J. Fenwick Young,
John S. Wright,
William Selden,
Theodore Roessle,
J. Maury Dove,
William F. Holtzman,
Charles Wheatley,
Levi Woodbury,
Henry A. Clarke,
George M. Oyster, Jr.,
Dr. Thomas O. Hill,
Dennis Connell,
J. E. Waugh,
W. H. A. Wormley,
Ch. Heurich,
E. P. Hickey,
Charles W. Pettit,
Frank P. Madigan,
Samuel Cross,
George T. Howard,
H. D. McIntyre,
R. F. Baker,
Thomas F. Miller,
Peter Fegan,
W. W. McCullough,
Thomas R. Benson,
George W. Harvey,
Daniel O'Brien,
C. C. Lancaster,
J. H. Johnson,
Gilbert Towles,
William H. Smith,
Charles Mades,
Walter Hawkes,

Dr. A. McWilliams,
John T. Hogan,
Dr. H. E. Leach,

W. J. Tune,
W. A. Croggin,
Dr. R. A. Bacon.

4. COMMITTEE ON PUBLIC ORDER,

To co-operate with the District Commissioners and the police department in reference to all matters pertaining to the good order of the city during the Inauguration.

N. D. Larner, Chairman,
C. W. Thorn,
Dr. W. O. Baldwin,
Thomas P. Morgan,
M. A. McGowan,
W. D. Peachy,
L. G. Hine,
Robert Ball,
Joseph Gawler,
L. Washington,
Geo. K. Thos. Dowling.
Alpheus Middleton,
T. W. Boteler,
W. J. Wilson,
Charles D. Liebeman,
F. D. Dowling,
N. O. Poole,
George Combs,
T. A. Rover,
John A. Ruff,
R. E. White,
H. P. Howard,
George R. Gray,

Wm. H. Morrison,
George W. Cochran,
O. C. Green,
Dr. James E. Morgan,
Dr. Charles Allen,
Dr. W. P. Young,
Maj. Wm. McE. Dye,
Edward Greaves,
John Keyworth,
Joseph Shillington,
Charles Walter,
John Boyle,
E. A. Ridgeway,
R. S. Fenwick,
F. W. Pratt,
Mayhew Plater,
M. C. Shuster,
I. L. Johnson,
J. Fenwick Young,
Julius Hugle,
Charles P. Williams,
H. T. Hudson.

5. COMMITTEE ON TRANSPORTATION,

To secure cheap rates of transportation to the city and to procure and furnish information thereof.

Henry L. Biscoe, Chairman,
Frank Hume,
George W. Knox,
Percy G. Smith,
Dr. Thos. B. Hammond,
Samuel G. Eberley,
C. C. Sailer,
L. L. Blake,
N. McDaniel,
P. Fleming,
William Wanstall,

Oscar A. Stevens,
George W. Moss,
L. Newmyer,
W. P. Welch,
George R. Phillips,
Lloyd R. Emmert,
Wash. Nailor,
R. C. Hewitt,
R. A. Parke,
T. W. Buckey,
William C. Murdock.

6. COMMITTEE ON CIVIC ASSOCIATIONS,

To ascertain and report what accommodations such associations can obtain.

Thos. J. Luttrell, Chairman,
John E. Norris,
W. A. Hutchins,

J. Hadley Doyle,
H. C. Clagett,
E. D. Wright,

J. C. Addison,
Joseph Hamlin,
Dr. C. P. Culver,
J. W. Arnold,
Dr. H. H. Barker,
Geo. W. Bauer,
B. T. Swart,
R. L. Cropley,
Bernard Kilmartin,
Jackson Yates,
James Goddard,
Julius Emner,
C. J. Butcher,
Benjamin F. Lloyd,
Joseph L. Coombs,
E. P. Berry,
Mills Dean,
J. H. O'Brien,
O. B. Dufour,
R. C. Glasscock,
Dr. Charles Allen,
W. H. Maginnis,
Charles S. Moore,
T. A. Robertson,
J. Fred. Kelley,
J. D. Entwistle,
W. A. Harkness,
R. J. Kennedy,
Daniel Loughran,
P. H. Christman,
R. E. Doyle,
Charles White,
J. B. Dayton,
James L. Falbey,
Clarence Hall,
A. A. Lipscomb,
Thomas F. Kelly,
H. G. Trader,
L. I. Dupre,
C. H. Fickling.
Dorsey Clagett,
Charles F. Rowe,
Edward Johnson,

Robert Callahan,
George T. Stewart,
W. P. Bell,
W. E. Dubant,
Harry W. Barbour,
Franklin Barrett,
Thomas Muntz,
W. H. Rose,
George W. Gaddis,
F H. Finley,
Charles F. Shelton,
L. Newmeyer,
Charles McLaughlin,
George J. Johnson,
George W. Donaldson,
W. O. Berry,
Maurice Splain,
John Dickson,
J T. Probey,
E. D. Lynch,
Thomas Cogan,
Dennis Connell,
J. Hall Colegate,
George Courtney,
Hezekiah Clagett,
John H. Cooney,
T. A. Hanson,
John J. Cook,
Hugh G. Divine,
P F. Cusick,
R. O. Edmonson,
John J. Hollister,
Julius Baumgarten,
Arthur Small,
John T. Green,
William H. Douglas,
Alvin Shuster,
Nathaniel Sardo,
Charles Thompson, Jr.,
M. J. Madegan,
Joseph Fanning,
John Leitch,
Dr. W. Bowie Tyler.

7. MILITARY ORGANIZATION COMMITTEE,

To ascertain and report what accommodations military associations may obtain.

Col. Wm. G. Moore, Chairman,
J. Tarbell Dyer,
Gen. S. B. Holabird,
Maj. Wm. B. Slack,
Capt. J. F. Oyster,
Col. George F. Timms,
Capt. B. R. Ross,
Capt. J. C. Entwistle,
Capt. Jas. E. Waugh,

Col. R. I. Fleming.
A. S. Worthington,
Lieut F. H. Harrington,
Capt. R. M. Rogers,
Capt. Levi Woodbury,
Col. Amos Webster,
M. M. Parker,
Col. Rob't Boyd,
E. S. Hutchinson,

E

Geo. E. Lemon,
Capt. C. A. Fleetwood,
Capt. T. S. Kelly,
Capt. D. M. Scott,
Lt. Geo. Mitchell,
J. V. W. Vandenbergh,
H. D. Cooke,
Col. J. G. Payne,
P. M. Dubant,
Charles Shafer,
A. T. Britton,
Capt. F. V. Greene,
James P. Ryon,
Jos. C. Lee,
James K. Cleary,
J. P. D. Phelps,
Robert Christy,
Gen. S. S. Henkle,
Richard C. Lewis,
Joseph Rickey,
Jas. C. Addison,
Allison Nailor,
Col. Chas. G. McCawley,
Gen. R. B. Ayers,
Col. A. Rockwell,
Capt. Wm. N. Dalton,
Capt. John S. Miller,
Capt. S. F. Thomasen,
Capt. M. E. Urell,
Lieut. J. O. Mansen,
Gen. Jas. M. Varnum,

Capt. H. Dingman,
Lieut. Geo. W. Evans,
Maj. C. Throckmorton,
Col. P. H. Allaback,
Gen. P. F. Bacon,
Wm. S. Roose,
Gen. H. L. Boughton,
Gen. J. A. Farnsworth,
Chas. W. Morgan,
M. J. Weller,
J. W. Drew,
Frank Hume,
Chris. Abner,
Carl Mueller,
Fillmore Beall,
Fred. Geseking,
Frank M. Lewis,
Andrew Saks,
Gen. Alb't Ordway,
Col. F. H. Smith,
Col. L. P. Wright,
Thos. Somerville,
Matthew Goddard,
Col. S. N. Benjamin,
Gen. B. H. Robertson,
F. P. Wright,
Capt. Geo. Breitbath,
Maj. C. B. Fisher,
Maj. H. L. Crawford,
Capt. G. A. Mushback,
R. C. Gwyn.

8. COMMITTEE ON ILLUMINATION,

To arrange for the illumination of the hall for the Inauguration Ball.

J. A. Baker, Chairman,
J. C. Ergood,
James L. Barbour,
Samuel Norment,
Watson Boyle,
James Wilkinson,
Charles B. Bailey,
Charles S. Bradley,
John F. Ennis,
W. H. Bailey.
Frank B. Mohun,
William B. Orme,
Robert M. Drinkard,
Thomas Russell,
Fred. W. Royce,

James L. Norris,
George A. McIlhaney,
James D. Clary,
B. H. Warner,
George W. Pearson,
John W Corson,
Charles G. Thorn,
W. H. H. Cissel,
N. H. Shea,
A. A. Hayes,
William H. Brawner,
John B. Larner,
Horatio Browning,
R. G. Campbell,

9. DECORATION AND MUSIC COMMITTEE,

To provide for the decoration of the hall, and for music.

E. G. Davis, Chairman,
Rr. Adm. J. L. Worden,
Edward Clarke,

Comd'r J. H Sands,
Comd'r C. F. Goodrich,
Comd'r R. P. Leary,

Com. J. G. Walker,
Com. W. S. Schley,
Samuel Ross,
Thos. B. Entwistle,
W. M. Poindexter,
Lieut. W. M. Wood,
J. L. Smithmeyer,
D. J. Macarty,
H. D Botclcr,
Julius Lansburgh,
Lloyd Moxley,
C. W. Howard,
W. L. Cowan,
E. F. Casey,
Henry C. McCauley,
William Wheatley,
Wm. F. Peddrick,
Benjamin Charlton,
Seaton Perry,
R. E. Leitch,
A. B. Mullett,
Charles C. Duncanson,
James F. Barbour,
Capt. Geo. W. Davis,
Pat. H. McLaughlin,
George Emmett, Jr.,
George T. Dunlop,
Edward Droop,
Lieut. T. B. M. Mason,
Lieut. R. P. Rodgers,
Paymaster Kenney,
Lieut. C. Pendleton,

C. E. Creecy,
J. R. Marshall.
Chas. A. Ball,
E. N. Gray,
B. B. Bradford,
John Saul.
John H. Small,
Wm. H. Hocke,
Chas. A. Harkness,
Gabriel Edmonston,
John Brady,
Chas. S. Denham,
Geo. T. Deering,
Edwin Harris,
Walter T. Wheatley,
S. H. Wimsatt,
G. A. Shehan,
Robert Portner,
Theo. J. Mayer,
Thomas J. Galt,
Chas. F. Schneider,
James D. Martin,
Chas. G. Ball,
C. W. Thorn,
John Cammack,
Edward Cammack,
J. V. N. Huyck,
Chas. H. Poor,
David Kindelberger,
A. M. Tubman,
J. Walter Paris,
Zephaniah Jones.

10. COMMITTEE ON FLOOR AND PROMENADE,

To take special charge of the Inauguration Ball, to receive the guests, and to carry into effect the programme of entertainment.

Wm. A. Gordon, Chairman,
Henry H. Dodge,
Woodbury Blair,
W. Cranch McIntire,
Maj. C. Throckmorton,
Reverdy Dangerfield,
Richard Smith,
Linden Kent,
H. E. Davis,
Calderon Carlisle,
Wm. A. McKenney,
Jesse Brown,
James B. Nalle,
Arthur T. Brice,
Ward Mohun,
Wm. H. Reeder, U. S. N.,
W. H. Scheutze, U. S. N.,
Frank Curtis, U. S. N.,
C. J. Badger, U. S. N.,
L. W. Piepmeyer, U. S. N.,

Arthur Padelford,
George W. Evans,
Walter A. Galt,
John M. Waters,
Robert Willett,
H. M. Norris,
Capt. R. M. Rodgers,
John Cochran,
Capt. J. F. Oyster,
Maj. A. S. Nicholson,
A. W. Francis,
William J. Acker,
Joseph Beardsley,
Frank J. Ward,
Jay Cooke,
Charles F. Schafer,
Frank B. Metzerott,
Charles McCawley,
John C. Poor,
Wm. Hayden Edwards,

Jacob G. Moore,
James M. Green,
Thomas N. Callan,
Dr. W. S. Harbin,
Dr. R. H. Goldsborough,
E. J. Stellwagen,
H. K. Willard,
H. H. Alexander,
Henry L. Bryan,
Randall Hagner,
R. H. Hazard,
William M. Dove,
Robert M. Larner,
George H. Kennedy,
W. Riley Deeble,
Samuel H. Wheeler,
J. Hiram Doyle,
M. C. Curtis,
John B. Trainer,
J. M. Johnston,
James Lowndes,
Wm. E. C. Moorhead,
P. L. Phillips,
F. W. Poor,
Randall Webb,
G. F. Appleby,
W. V. R. Berry,
Sevellon A. Brown,
George B. Emory,
Joseph Dodson,
Charles Hill,
Augustus Jay,
H. Q. Keyworth,
Harry H. Ellis,
O. I. Meek,
William R. Keyworth,
F. E. Alexander,
Robert Leding,
John C. Wilson,
Howard C. Russell,
Ed. F. Hosmer,
Howard Boteler,
J. Blake Kendall,
Orlando G. Wales,
William C. Myers,
H. Clay Stewart, Jr.,
Frank D Middleton,
Francis Tonncy,
Robert S. Chew,
A. H. Parris,
Lieut. W. H. Slack,
John G. Thompson,
J. S. Larcombe,
J. H. Cragin,
John H. Magruder,
C. R. McBlair,
Gen. B. Robertson,
J. J. Darlington,

T. A. Lambert,
Blair Lee,
Wm. H. Phillips,
T. L. Holbrook,
Charles A. Elliott,
Harry S. Barbour,
J. H. Patrick,
E. B. Hay,
R. O. Holtzman,
Frank G. Middleton,
Ensign T. S. Rogers,
Charles S. Moore,
F. T. Browning,
Irvine G. Ashby,
F. B. Noyes,
Charles H. Ruoff,
Harrison H. Dodge,
A. B. Cropley,
Howard Goodrich,
W. T. Wheatley,
Charles E. Galt,
C. H. Smith,
Galt Davis,
W. Lenox Towers,
T. C. Quantrell,
Charles Cropley,
J. Edwin Wilson,
S. N. Woodward,
L. G. Marini,
Ralph L Galt,
William C. Hill,
Samuel Maddox,
T. L. Riggs,
Ross Thompson,
J. H. Gordon,
Dr. T. F. McArdle,
Dr. H. E. Leach,
Thomas M. Gale,
George Gibson Colgate,
W. O. N. Scott,
Thomas C. Hungerford,
Charles P. Williams,
F. E. Middleton,
William B. Boteler,
John A. Downs,
David Rittenhouse,
C. C. Bryan,
James E. Wilkins,
W. W. Greenfield,
John Hollister,
Davis Shepherd,
Cazenove G. Lee,
H. F. Bauer,
Frank B. Loving,
Dr. William May,
Seaton Munroe,
Woodbury Loring,
Clifford Richardson,

C. Wyckliffe Yulee,
Henry Adams,
John J. Chew,
John Davis,
Maj. T. B. Ferguson,
A. B Briggs,
A. Tyssowski,
William Lay,
J. L. Robertson,
A. Crane, Jr.,
John Ancona,
Percy Hills,
John W. Sims,
Joseph O. Brawner,

Frank S. Parks,
J. H. Wardle,
T. C. Crawford,
Philip F. Larner,
F. B. Hempstone,
Norval L. Burchell,
Richard F. Pairo,
Harry B. Parker,
C. J. Butcher,
William H Beck,
Samuel C. Wilson,
Norman Bestor,
W. H. French, Boston.

11. COMMITTEE ON PRESS,

To make suitable arrangements for the members of the press.

F. A. Richardson, Chairman,
George W. Adams,
O. O. Stealey,
C. S. Noyes,
I. N. Burritt,
Charles Nordhoff,
F. A. G. Handy,
Gen. H. V. Boynton,
John M. Carson,
James R. Young,
C. L. Towle,
M. D. Helm,
T. B. Kalbfus,
H. L. West,
O. P. Austin,
C. T. Murray,
Louis Schade,
W. L. MacFarland,
E. G. Dunnell,

R. H. Sylvester,
L. Q. Washington,
Ben. Perley Poore,
T. C. Crawford,
Edmund Hudson,
W. C. MacBride,
W. B. Shaw,
H. J. Ramsdell,
Frank P. Morgan,
J. V. Cracraft,
Watson Boyle,
Harold Snowden,
A. J. Clarke,
Dr. F. T. Howe,
George E. Gilliland,
P. V. DeGraw,
T. G. Morrow,
Daniel Leech,
J. B. McCarthy.

12. SPECIAL SUB-COMMITTEE,

To have supervision of all the other committees under the general direction of this body.

Wm. M. Galt,
Gen. C. M. McKeever,
Thomas J. Fisher,
A. A. Wilson,
Wm. H. Clagett,
Lawrence Gardner,
James P. Willett,

Admiral D. D. Porter,
Stilson Hutchins,
Samuel V. Niles,
Curtis J. Hillyer,
H. A. Willard,
F. B. McCuire,
Thomas J. Luttrell.

The Chairman of this body will be ex-officio chairman of each of the foregoing twelve sub-committees, and shall have power to fill vacancies therein.

The undersigned recommend the persons whose names are hereto annexed as proper persons to compose the several sub-committees. Respectfully submitted,

JAMES F. BERRET, CHARLES C. GLOVER, M. F. MORRIS, WILLIAM M. GALT, A. A. WILSON, *Committee.*

GEORGE WASHINGTON.

MRS. CUSTIS.

When the appointed hour arrives, it is supposed that three guns will be fired, to apprise the different companies, societies, organizations and clubs that it is time to form in line, as the procession is to move precisely at 10.30 A. M. It will form on the Avenue, near 20th street, with its right flank resting on South 20th, 19th and 18th streets, and will be composed of citizens in full dress. The left flank will rest on North 20th, 19th and 18th streets, and consist of the United States regulars and light infantry companies from different States, commanded by General Hancock, aided by General George B. McClellan. In the front two battalions of cavalry. Then grand marshal and aids, followed by a band of music. The centre will be made up of Chief Justice Waite and Associate Justices, in carriage, drawn by four white horses. The marine band. President Arthur escorting Grover Cleveland and Thomas Hendricks, in his private carriage drawn by six horses. National Executive Committee in carriages drawn by four horses.

Distinguished guests in carriages. Sena-
tors, and also Representatives in carriages,
followed by the distinguished citizens and
different organizations.

When the line is ready to march a signal
will be given, by the firing of cannon.

The procession, when ready to march,
will be composed of as fine a lot of men as
ever marched in line. It is expected that
there will be not less than five hundred
companies, clubs and organizations from
the different cities of the nation. Already
the headquarters for the different companies have been engaged. When the procession arrives at the Capitol, Chief Justice
Waite will escort Cleveland and Hendricks
into the Senate chamber, when Thomas
Hendricks will be sworn in as Chairman of
the Senate. When this is done they will
then march to the place prepared for the
Inaugural Address of our next President,
where Chief Justice Waite will administer
the oath of office, as follows :—

" You, Grover Cleveland, President-elect
of the United States of America, do solemnly

swear, in presence of Almighty God, that
you will support the Constitution of the
United States, and also the Statutes of the
District of Columbia, and that you will well
and truly perform your duties as President
of the United States, to the best of your
ability.   So help you God.

Mr. Cleveland will then kiss the Bible,
and he will be President of the United
States, for all its people. He will then
deliver his Inaugural Address. When this is
done they will return to their carriages and
march back to the White House in the same
order as in coming, when President Cleveland will review the different companies and
organizations. They will then disband and
dinner will be next in the order of the day.
Afterward the time will be occupied by preparations for the Reception and Promenade
Concert in the evening, which will be
opened as early as nine o'clock, and there
will be one of the finest displays of beauty,
health and wealth ever congregated in
America.

THE INAUGURATION BALL.

It is decided that this will be held in the area of the new Pension building, which will be fitted up for the occasion, and when completed, will make a large and convenient ball-room. It contains 36,656 square feet, and will be elaborately decorated with bunting of the United States colors, and draped with curtains of rich damask. Each State will exhibit its emblem and a shield, with its motto.

It is expected that Grover Cleveland, the President, will make his appearance during the evening, accompanied by one of New York's most accomplished ladies. There is some talk of sending a special invitation to the Princess of Lorne and her husband, the Governor General of Ontario. Should they accept, the people of Washington will enjoy the privilege of seeing a live princess in their midst. Ladies will come from every State in the Union, and there will be a greater display of beauty and wealth than has ever been witnessed on this continent, and perhaps, in the world. Let us hope that nothing will occur to mar the pleasure of any one, no matter how humble, who may attend.

The costumes of the ladies will be a noted feature of this occasion. Many, no doubt, will appear in walking suits, but the majority will wear elaborate and handsome toilets. I have a description of some of them from a celebrated establishment in Washington, which may prove interesting and instructive to my lady readers.

One of them is for a blonde, made of pale blue silk, with white lace for the draperies and trimmings; red peonies are worn on the bodice, and knots of wide blue satin ribbon mingle with the lace on the train; pearl ornaments. Another is of coral pink; the front of the skirt made of embroidered pink plush, with cascades of languedoc on either side; the train and bodice are of pink duchesse satin, the latter cut square in the neck and embroidered with plush flowers; diamond and pearl necklace.

A sapphire blue velvet has a skirt of pale blue duchesse satin, trimmed diagonally with point lace, alternated with satin pleating. The train and bodice are of velvet, with point lace on the latter.

The skirt of a mauve dress is of pale yellow shot silk, trimmed with white gauze plaitings. Its upper portion is almost entirely veiled with gauze, trimmed with point appliqué lace, and the draperies are caught here and there with large clusters of tea roses. The train and low bodice are of mauve merveilleaux satin, clusters of mauve ribbon and tea roses adorning the latter. A small bunch of tea roses is worn in the hair, and an opal necklace around the neck.

One of the dresses most pleasing to my taste is of heliotrope duchesse satin ; the skirt is trimmed with alternate flounces of point lace and satin ; the front drapery is caught up on one side, and ornamented by a cascade of lace, interspersed with bows of narrow ribbon, and beside it a cluster of pond lilies; the bodice is decollete, with a rich fall of lace; the train is of satin, with a mass of lilies thrown on one side.

A rich costume is made of white satin and velvet; the front of the skirt is of white satin, with embroidered figures of royal purple velvet; the train and pointed bodice are of purple velvet, the latter cut low, and half filled in with crushed roses of the most delicate pink shade; a necklace of diamonds with pendant is worn, and long gloves.

A very handsome dress, suitable for a brunette, is one of black duchesse satin, covered with black tulle. The bodice is cut pompadour, and adorned with marigolds, a cluster of which also holds the tulle drapery in place on the skirt. Amber jewels will be most appropriate.

A light-red ribbed-velvet dress would be very becoming to one of our Southern ladies. The velvet train falls in rich folds, while the front of the skirt is crossed by two scarf draperies of pink silk gauze. One is looped high on the hip, meeting the other, which is caught up high on the left side and held very low on the right by a cluster of red ostrich tips. The closely-fitting bodice, also of velvet, is trimmed with gauze and a bouquet of ostrich tips. A bunch of these is fastened in the hair, and the jewels worn are diamonds.

I cannot pass unnoticed a costume made of yellow satin; the skirt and bodice are entirely covered with Spanish lace, and the scarf drapery is held in place with bunches of chrysanthemums. The bodice is similarly adorned, and amber ornaments will be used.

For a young lady, there is one both novel and pretty; the skirt is of white silk, covered with white point lace flounces, on which are thrown clusters of black ostrich tips with aigrette; the train, bodice and drapery are of coral pink brocade, a cluster of black feathers holding the latter on the right hip; the bodice has a high collar softened by a fall of lace. A bunch of black feathers adorn the hair, and pearl ornaments are worn.

There is a charming costume of white silk and gauze, for a debutante. The skirt is trimmed with plaiting, headed with a garland of pale pink flowers. The gauze drapery is adorned in a similar manner, with flowers, as also the bodice, which is gauze, striped lengthwise with bands of satin. The back drapery of gauze forms a pouf at the top, and falls to the end of the train, veiling the flowers. A cluster of pink roses, with aigrette is worn in the hair. Long snede gloves and pearl ornaments complete this dainty toilet.

Another is of cream-colored satin, with a pearl front in the skirt; the paniers are of satin, with a deep border of pearl trimming and point lace; the train and bodice are of satin; the latter decollete, ornamented by flowers. These are blush pinks or carnations, and made into a half wreath, worn across the front of the bodice, and placed between the lace which borders the edge and a band of pearl trimming. A very small cluster of the pinks or carnations is worn a little below the left ear, in the hair, when it is coiled low, and is very becoming to young ladies with classical shaped heads.

Then I find one made of surah silk, a new shade, called peachblow. It would be suitable for a miss in her teens, and make a lovely dress trimmed with Oriental lace; the bodice is cut half low and the arms bare, each ornamented with a pearl necklace, twisted like a double bracelet around the wrist.

Perhaps the most interesting portion of my list is that of the bridal costumes. One of them is made of Marie Louise blue velvet and cream-colored silk. The back of the dress is of the velvet, made princesse style. The front of the skirt and bodice are one, made of satin; the former festooned with silver tissue, caught here and there with knots of arbutus. The bodice is cut low and half filled in with the tissue fastened by sprays of arbutus. A necklace of diamonds and opals is worn.

Another is of white satin, with cascades of point lace down the front, caught up by tiny pearl buckles. The bodice is cut square

F

and filled in with lace fastened at the throat with a pearl clasp.

A mauve-colored moire antique has a long train draped on the point of the bodice, in such a manner as to show facings of a delicate pink shade.   Sprays of apple blossoms are thrown on the skirt, and also adorn the bodice, which is cut "V" shaped, and filled in with crêpe lisse dotted with pink.

Some of the reception toilets display such richness of material and perfection of taste, that I cannot pass them by unnoticed.

Among many, there is one worthy of special mention.   I call it "the pansy costume."   It is made of deep violet silk, cut with a close-fitting bodice ; the skirt is of violet satin, brocaded with velvet pansies, outlined with threads of gold ; the train is of silk, as also the full paniers, which are trimmed with pansies, transposed and held in place by golden threads.   The bodice has a high Medici collar, both sides of the opening ornamented with a tiny pansy.

At the left side, and near the waist, is fastened a large bunch of velvet pansies with golden hearts.

There is a handsome pale blue brocade, with a train and bodice of pink plush; a shower of duchesse lace covers the front of the skirt, and the bodice is trimmed with a fall of the same.

Then I notice a dress of cameo pink cashmere, with pleatings on the skirt, headed with a double row of swan's down; the drapery is also trimmed with this fur; likewise the bodice, which is cut square in the neck. A double necklace of pearls is worn, and an opera cloak to match the suit in color and trimming, is thrown over the shoulders.

A pretty toilet is one made of a shade of green satin, called "sea foam," having a long Watteau back, extending from the collar down to the end of the train, in rich and graceful folds. The front is trimmed with point lace and a scattering of rosebuds. The bodice is open, and ornamented by a half-garland of fragrant Jacqueminot roses.

And now remain the walking suits, which merit, perhaps, as much attention as any of the others.

Among the favorite combinations, are smoke-gray, with garnet velvet; crimson plaid, with black and often new shades of silk, with velvet to match. Of the latter, is one in gray Ottoman silk; the skirt is trimmed with ruchings and plaitings; the tablier is of velvet brocade to match the silk, and slashed into panels, with plaiting of silk in between; the back drapery of silk is fastened over the point of the bodice, which is trimmed with a band of brocade on either side, narrowing to a point at the waist. A lace jabot completes the costume.

An elegant suit is of dark blue velvet, the polonaise tunic open in front and trimmed with feathers, which extend to the throat and around the neck, also ornamenting the wrists.

A very pretty suit is made of heavy corded silk; the skirt hangs in box plaits, each ornamented at the bottom with an odd design of passementerie trimming; the drapery has a scarf in front, held higher on one side than the other, and very bouffant at the back. The bodice shows a plastron gathered into a half rest, and has a high Medici collar; a daisy rosette of narrow ribbon, with a centre of a brighter color, is placed on the left side of the collar, and one on the right side of the rest.

Another quiet but handsome costume is of brown velvet; the skirt trimmed, to the depth of a foot, in golden beaver fur. The jacket is of brown plush, with a short cape of the same, trimmed in fur. A fur collar and. cuffs complete the suit.

Cashmere is handsomely combined with plaid when it matches one of the colors in the changeable fabric; it is also used with plain material, and, with skill and ingenuity, can be made to look sometimes richer than silk, and far preferable.

HOW TO DRESS FOR THE OCCASION.*

For full dress, for gentlemen, black swallow-tail coat, single breasted; rolling collar; open low, with three buttons. Trousers, black; formed to leg. Pearl silk tie; standing collar. Gloves same shade of tie. Diamonds or pearl studs in bosom.

Gentlemen who escort ladies to the Ball can accommodate their dress to their ladies' costumes. With ladies in street costume, or what we term semi-dress, gentlemen can, with propriety, wear the Prince Albert coat, dark plum, blue, green or black; vest, same material; trousers of some dark pin stripe or check goods. Gloves cream kids. Tie black or cream silk.

The above styles are laid down by the fashionable tailors of New York, Boston, Philadelphia and Washington.

* H. D. Barr, Washington, D. C.

"OUR SHIP OF STATE."

I.

This glorious governmental craft so strong and long
    has stood,
Her frame must be of iron made, and of the best of
    wood ;
She has had for her captains many a brave and goodly
    man,
And as they go before we'll replace them best we
    can.

II.

In all her stormy adventures, which captains generally
    dread,
Kind Providence has so provided that she has come
    out ahead.
The Republicans have newly rigged her out, and
    she is so neat a boat,
That with fifty million people, she has no trouble to
    float.

III.

But there always are some people that have so much
    to say,
And how soon they raised their voices—" You're
    steering the wrong way ! "

The Democrats began to warble, and on that story
    long did dwell ;
And others made the assertion, she was not managed
    well !

IV.

And many a scandal there was really being told,
Of how the Republican leaders were stealing of our
    gold.
They all harangued, and shouted, " Let's turn the
    rascals out ; "
And that is, perhaps, the reason the Republican defeat
    came about.

V.

Consequently, to this craft a new captain will be sent,
After a long and weary campaign, with time and
    money spent ;
And when on the 4th of March the captain and his
    mate will come,
You will hear the firing of the cannon, and the beating
    of the drum.

VI.

The Inauguration will be conducted with a very great
    display,
When Grover Cleveland will be the Hero of the day !
Chief Justice Waite will administer to him the oath
(It never has been customary, so he will not swear
    in both).

VII.

Then Chester Arthur will deliver the papers in his
    hand,
When Grover Cleveland, our President, will take
    the ship's command,
And we hope he'll call around him the best men
    of the State,
Alive Americans we hope they'll be, for the dead*
    ones we do hate.

VIII.

Then, after a thorough search, he will pick there-
    from his crew,
And gently wave his hand, and say that that will
    do.
Then he will tell his first mate, Bayard, or some
    other man,
"Order your men to the halyards, and do as I com-
    mand;

IX.

" The gale may spring upon us, and we cannot tell
    how quick,
For I notice in yon horizon, the clouds look dark
    and thick."
He then will to his cabin go, take down the old
    worn chart,
"I must make no mistake in this voyage," says he,
    "I feel it in my heart."

* Dead in trespasses and sin.

X.

Next day the Treasurer of the ship will spread his
books out wide,
And say, "My dear Mr. President, it's for you to
decide
Whether we've done our duty, as servants to the
people,
Or whether we, as brigands, should hang on yonder
steeple."

XI.

Mr. President will then put on his glasses, and ex-
amine long and well;
What the result will be, my reader, will be hard for
me to tell.
But I will not allow myself on these men to reflect;
I hope, in every instance, their books will be correct;
And that there has not been one dollar allowed to
go astray,
Neither has there any gold been carried or stole away.

XII.

If this view is correct, which I think will be the
case,
'Twill surely save much trouble, and the Republicans
from disgrace;
And, when after this search is made, should there
prove to be no sin,
The Civil Service Bill should keep its worthy
servants in.

XIII.

Now the Chief will light his cigarette, and on the
    deck will walk,
Consulting with his officers in a long and earnest
    talk.
He will then take a voyage on the glassy depths of
    time,
And will bring the ship to harbor, when he hears the
    golden chime ;
And he will cast her anchor in the Great Jehovah's
    Bay,
Where our good Lord will watch her, and keep her
    foes away.

XIV.

Our old flag will be flying from the mast's highest top ;
If any one dare touch it, he on the spot will drop ;
And on our ensign will be written, " We never say
    fail—''
Our free institutions shall ever prevail.

THOMAS H. BENTON.   DANIEL WEBSTER.   JOHN C. CALHOUN.

HENRY CLAY.   STEPHEN A. DOUGLASS.

SALMON P. CHASE.   HORACE GREELEY.   Wm. H. SEWARD.

HOW A LIFE SHOULD BE SPENT

TO ATTAIN THE GREATEST AMOUNT OF TRUE HAPPINESS, BY A NATION OR INDIVIDUAL.

———

That which is worth living for is worth preserving; but in a great many cases this seems to be entirely forgotten. In how many instances do we find that after men have attained high positions, they become vain, and in their actions thereafter, seem to discountenance those who helped them. This immediately destroys all the confidence of their fellow men, and in less time than it took them to obtain their position, do they lose it. If our public men wish to avoid disappointment, they should cherish our country and have respect for its subjects.

The love of country or home is as strong, if not stronger than most all other passions in the human breast; for in a country favored like America, all the beauties of manhood are developed in their pure Christian spirit,

93

and by the freedom of its institutions man is elevated to a social and Christian position.

The beauties of a true life consist of true fellowship with pure motives. No man, woman or child can afford to give his or her time to the wily ways of the Evil One, in trying to enjoy him or herself in a life of impure motives.

In trying to impress these truths on my readers, I have endeavored to prove them, and to illustrate the subject so clearly that there will be no misapprehension.

If life is worth living, it is best to derive from it solid comfort, and such things as do not feed cankerous worms of regret, which are an annoyance, and which will stay with you until the end of time; throw aside all conscience, and perhaps they will be silenced until the breakers are heard on the other shore. They will then rise up in their fury and occupy the place of their inhabitation, and the full realization of a misspent life will come up before you. Every sin, whether of a nation or an individual, will find him or it out; or, in other words, your sins will find you out.

It is written that, in the Last Day, the Books will be opened. My reader, did you ever think who was the book-keeper? You are this book-keeper, and you cannot destroy that book; it is written with indelible ink, and time will not erase it.

All the men of noted wickedness in high positions have felt remorse. Charles IX made the remark to his doctor, "O, if I had spared the innocent." How many of the Crowned Heads would have given their kingdoms for a horse, to flee from the wrath that they had heaped upon their own heads. But you cannot flee from a conscience of regret. It will remain with you always, and then will come the full realization of a misspent and worthless life.

The love of life is tenaciously inherent in all animate creatures, and, in my judgment and observation, the being that is most innocent seems to have the least trouble, even with its foes ; just so with the human family or a nation.

The man or woman who leads the most innocent and virtuous life has the least difficulty with conflicts of evil thoughts and actions.

The power of love was never intended to be cast away for destruction, no more than pearls before swine; but, on the contrary, it was meant for those who would appreciate and reciprocate it. Therefore, in the first tuition of the rising generations, the great object should be to teach them to love those that have noble principles and pure motives. As the mineral crops out in the regions of its interior wealth, so good or evil motives crop out in the child ; and, as children are generally quick of perception, they should be taught to shun all society that is deceptive, and of low moral habits, for when children once form these associations, the tendency toward them is very detrimental to their future happiness.

The love that goes to comfort life is that which is pure, and that which does not allow itself to be trespassed upon. The first principles of self-protection and happiness are: love to do good, a desire for pure motives, and contentment of mind, through the knowledge of having led a life of true charity.

This is something all wish to claim, and my object in this work is twofold: that I may benefit the nation, through its subjects.

It is written, in the Book of all books, that the pure in heart shall inherit the Kingdom of God. These words must be true, and no one dares to deny them, for in man the principles of right and wrong are firmly rooted; this also cannot be denied with sincerity.

Then, if these two truths, which agree, open the way to happiness and glory, why not train your children to adopt them?

There are a great many seeds of diseases that try to find root in the human family, but I do not discover in any of them a worse foe than remorse, for in different afflictions there is a time of rest; but regret never ceases, for it has its victims sure, and the more evil seed the more the victim suffers. Then, why not begin at the proper

G

time, and let children know the evils for them
to shun, and teach them that true happiness
consists in self-preservation, and the love to
do good to those who are worthy of their
confidence and charity.

Some men live in this world for self entirely, as if it was made for them exclusively,
going through it without principle or honor,
only seeking those they can use for their
own aggrandizement and selfish purposes.

But such people are not happy, and
utterly devoid of Christian love.

Love has a truer motive; it gives contentment of mind, and endows those who cultivate it with the knowledge of true happiness.   The fruit of well doing is expanded
by constant practice. It is a virtue that
sheds rays of light and happiness around
all circles and associations. Let a nation
or neighborhood consist of those who have
no love for its subjects, and I will show you
a nation which has a constant amount of
strife, trouble, war and crime.   However, it
is not necessary to mention any, for they
are too well known to be unobserved.

The crowned heads of Europe have not shown much love for their subjects, but, on the contrary, have used many good methods to govern them for their own safety and comfort. War generally follows aristocracy, anarchy and tyranny.

Happiness and comfort follow love, respectability, industry and progress.

In the beginning of manhood or womanhood, the great object in view should be to learn how to live, and to be of the most use, to yourself, friend, fellow man and country.

Many people do not consider the future, its hopes, fears, and the consequence of its gains and losses, but, without a moment of necessary reflection, dive into its wondrous depths; consequently the results are often different from those they first expected. In the first instance, fathom your place of plunging before you take the leap; also see that there is no rock or quagmire to wreck your future prospects.

It is short work to take these precautions; nevertheless, how often are they

neglected. For an illustration: I once saw
a gentleman who was, from all appearances,
an intellectual man, and worth not less
than a half a million of dollars; his wife,
in her own right, had a million, and they
were visiting the seaside with two or three
children. They got ready for a bath, and
all seemed delighted with the prospect;
but how soon their expectations vanished!
The father, immediately on going into the
water, waded to a boat that was tied near,
and entered it, where the water was not
waist deep, and he plunged head foremost
into the shallow water. The consequence
was that, his head coming in contact with
the hard sand and pebbles, he was severely
injured. All the pleasure which they had
just begun to enjoy was turned into sor-
row, and, if I am not mistaken, he carries
the mark of that accident to this day.
One forethought and all might have been
averted.

Just so in the daily walks of life; we
should first ask if it is prudent, and if we
answer ourselves truthfully, we may, nine

times out of ten, avoid many difficulties. How many accidents occur simply by want of thought, and not keeping ourselves on our guard. Take, for instance, the accidents that happen by the cars running over people at the crossings ; a great many would not occur if they would take one moment to reflect. Men seem like geese in their actions. How many times, in my travels through life, have I seen these web-footed birds on the highway, and on the approach of a wagon, most invariably would you see one or more of the flock cross the track ; in thousands of instances, if they succeeded in so doing, they would immediately stop and flap their wings; but a great many of these do not succeed in the perilous attempt. Just so with men. How often have I seen, when the cars are coming, young and old want to cross the track, and as soon as they have done so, at once stop, turn and look at the monstrous train that would have crushed out their life in an instant, had they only made one misstep. In ninety-nine times out of one hundred of such instances, have I seen the railroad managers blamed, while, in fact, it is the fault of those who are foolhardy enough to risk their limbs and life so carelessly. There is always plenty of time to let the train pass, although so few remember this.

If you, my readers, will search, you will find enough in this subject for a guide to health, wealth and happiness.

There is such a thing as losing your chance of success by too much reflection, for while you contemplate and meditate, your opportunity sometimes vanishes.

But every man, as I have said before, has that principle of right and wrong so indelibly imprinted on his mind, that it does not require but a moment to understand his situation.

Then take this for your motto, my dear reader: "Look, before you leap;" which is old, but sure; and when the placid waters of the future are reached, and you want to cross them safely, before you do so, have immediate thought of your life and happiness when you enter the frail boat to cross. The wind may rise, the tide may be strong, and your captain may be a gay deceiver, who only wishes to get where he can carry you to destruction for his own advantage.

There is a very good road that leads to the wharf of safety, and it is called "through by daylight." Whatever road you take to happiness, be sure of this: that you are not afraid to let the world know you are on the Public Highway, and not in the dark lanes and alleys. Be sure to shun those who flatter you; and also beware, when you come in contact with a person, ever so good looking or well dressed, who desires to take you out of the highway into the valley beneath; you may rest assured that he wishes to advance some idea or action that he does not wish the world or your friends to know. What is done by respectable and law-abiding citizens, is done openly, and with no fear of reproach or scrutiny. If it is a business transaction, you will find them ready for criticism.

There are thousands of ways in this world to enjoy life, and these all honorable ones. There are also a thousand and one other ways that lead to discord, unhappiness, crime, poverty, destruction and death. So, my dear readers, shun every thought, deed or action that will take you from the one great thought of happiness.

Pride is sometimes spoken of in a light way, such as, "pride must have a fall;" but I would not, for a moment, say one word against it. It is a word in its proper place, and a passion that our God has bestowed upon us, as a great and good guide to happiness, for without it what would be the history of this nation and its people? The son or daughter who have no pride and self-respect, will, sooner or later, be extremely mortified to find that they have attained maturity devoid of so important a characteristic.

Vanity belongs to those that have time to take charge of it; but pride is just the thing to make a boy and girl grow up to be a man or woman of use and benefit to

their country and fellow-neighbors. The
boy that has pride will shun his inferiors;
and the girl that has pride will some time
make a lady of refinement and culture, a
good sister, a loving wife, and a fond
mother.

There is nothing worse than vanity, for
it puffs itself up, and, of course, there must
be an end to inflation. Necessarily, an
explosion occurs. Vanity is never too high
to stoop to do any low or mean thing to
accomplish its object. Not so with pride;
it elevates the mind; keeps the body clean
and tidy; and, as a general thing, uses
economy. It also provides a way for the
cultivation of its children, and finds help to
educate the nation; lifts up the fallen, and
supplies the wants of the poor. A man
will not allow himself to be dejected, for
that very reason: pride will fly to the rescue,
and make an appeal that he cannot resist;
nature springs forth to action at once; the
situation is comprehended, and the remedy
immediately applied, in every case a true
one, for self-respect and pride will at once

exert themselves, and the two combined will bring the victory.

Then cultivate this virtue, and let every statesman or schoolboy learn to know that if he is ever to be a gentleman he must, necessarily, have pride to assist him in his purpose.

No man holding a general responsibility can afford to be caught in the slums of darkness, either by himself or others; for if he himself knows it, he will, in some future time upbraid himself for it.

Bad company is not a good thing to keep, for as the worm of regret turns itself over in a man's brain, it very often disturbs its keeper, and every man holding a high position will be brought to account for his stewardship, according to his responsibility.

Thousands of watchers are constantly on the alert to catch and ape the actions of our public men. Then let them beware what examples they set to the rising generation and world at large, which only wait for an example, and whether it be good or bad, it

goes out to the world as it is sent, only to
be tenfold in its manifestations.

Therefore, I would say, so that I may not
be misunderstood, do not cultivate vice nor
touch anything that will pollute your innocent hands; nor must you allow those that
would have a tendency to draw you away
from virtue to influence you, nor even to
touch the hem of your garment; if you do
so, they will corrupt you, financially or
morally. The words used on the Mount,
"Get thee behind me, Satan," should ever
be your watchword.

I have attended a great many different
exhibitions of fine arts, sculpture, delicate
mechanisms, and beautiful handwork in
laces of great value, and in passing I have
remarked two large words standing for the
protection of them: "Hands off!" How
effectually these words could be applied to
a great many in the daily walks of life.

My dear reader, have you never thought
that you are of more value to your parents
than the finest work of art? If this be so
in respect to those who have watched over

you, and with joy have seen your first footsteps, do display these words in every action of your life, by a firm lip and a determined eye.

There is only one way to get rid of remorse, and that is by going to Jesus ; through Him and Him alone can your conscience be freed from the worm of regret ; and the time to go to Him is the present.

Do not listen to that voice of procrastination. It will carry you too far, as it is a friend to remorse, and you will ever suffer the pangs of regret, and only awake to a full sense of your condition when it is too late. There is no remedy when the other shore is reached. Your chance is lost forever ; weeping will avail naught. Only to be happy in the love of Jesus will save you.

Christianity does not make your pleasures less, but gives you such as do not feed the worm, that never dieth. Now is the time to prepare to live, and when you are ready to live a pure life before your God and fellow man, then can you rejoice, for you have a sound foundation on which to rejoice.

Then do not prepare to die. There is no such thing as death, but life everlasting, or eternal remorse; which is worse than death, as its torments never cease.

Then go to Him who suffered and bled for you, that you might through Him receive the gift of everlasting life, which through folly and sin you had lost. To-day He waits with outstretched arms to receive you, but to-morrow the clouds may rise and your opportunity be lost; forever lost!

> " Of all the words of tongue or pen,
> The saddest ones, it might have been."

FINANCIAL CONDITION OF
OUR COUNTRY.

This country was never in a better financial condition than at the present. There are large amounts of silver and gold in the Treasury. The grand total of gold and silver held by the Treasury, national and private banks on the first day of November, is shown by the following table, as reported by the Comptroller of the currency:

Gold coin and bullion	$585,611,872
Silver coin	275,735,439
Legal-tender notes	346,681,016
National Bank notes	333,559,813

There has been no change in the aggregate of legal-tender notes outstanding, which still remains as fixed by the Act of May 31st, 1878. National Bank notes have decreased $18,453,974 during the year. The amounts of gold and silver have increased $3,641,618, and $33,033,507, respectively, making the total increase during the year in gold, silver and currency, $18,221,151.

The table annexed gives the portion of the gold, silver and currency held by the United States Treasury, and by the national and State banks. The amounts in the United States Treasury are for the corresponding dates with those in the preceding table. The amounts in the national banks are for the corresponding dates nearest thereto on which returns were made to the Comptroller, viz: January 1, 1879; October 1, 1881; October 3, 1882; October 2, 1883; and September 30, 1884. The amounts in the State banks, trust companies and savings banks have been compiled from official reports for the nearest obtainable dates.

	January 1, 1879.	November 1, 1881.	November 1, 1882.	November 1, 1883.	November 1, 1884.
GOLD.					
In the Treasury, less certificates	$112,703,342	$167,781,909	$148,435,473	$157,353,760	$134,670,790
In national banks, including certificates	35,039,201	107,222,169	94,127,324	97,570,057	117,185,407
In State banks, including certificates	10,937,812	19,901,491	17,892,500	18,255,300	25,928,757
Total gold	158,680,355	294,905,569	260,455,297	273,179,117	277,784,954
SILVER.					
In the Treasury, standard silver dollars	$17,249,740	$66,576,378	$92,414,977	$116,036,450	$142,926,725
In the Treasury, bullion	9,321,417	3,424,575	4,012,503	4,936,365	4,646,497
In the Treasury, fractional coin	6,048,194	25,984,687	26,749,482	26,712,424	29,346,757
In national banks	6,460,557	7,112,567	8,234,739	10,247,926	8,592,557
Total silver	38,879,908	103,098,207	131,411,701	157,933,165	185,012,536

CURRENCY.	January 1, 1879.	November 1, 1881.	November 1, 1882.	November 1, 1883.	November 1, 1884.
In the Treasury, less certificates	$44,425,655	$22,774,830	$26,224,248	$30,996,217	$26,258,827
In national banks, including certificates	126,491,720	77,630,917	92,544,767	103,316,809	114,507,113
In State banks, including certificates	25,944,485	27,391,317	27,086,482	28,259,062	32,659,605
In savings banks	14,513,779	11,782,243	14,724,978	12,998,594	14,079,452
Total currency	211,375,639	139,579,307	160,580,475	175,570,682	187,504,997
Grand totals	408,935,902	537,583,083	552,447,473	606,682,964	550,302,487

If the aggregates of gold, silver and currency for the several dates in the above table be deducted from the amounts of the same items at corresponding dates in the table which precedes it, the remainders will be, approximately, the amounts in the hands of the people at corresponding dates.

	January 1, 1879.	November 1, 1881.	November 1, 1882.	November 1, 1883.	November 1, 1884.
Gold	$119,629,771	$256,016,829	$286,900,965	$308,791,137	$307,826,918
Silver	67,693,895	78,377,937	77,332,723	84,768,767	90,722,903
Currency	459,097,051	567,445,959	548,828,288	523,124,121	492,735,832
Total	646,420,717	901,840,725	913,061,976	916,684,025	891,285,653

The gold in the Treasury, including bullion in the process of coinage, has decreased during the year $22,682,970, and in the banks has increased $27,288,807. The paper currency in the Treasury has decreased $4,737,390, and in the banks has increased $16,671,605. The decrease of gold outside of the Treasury and the banks has been $964,219, and of silver coin $5,954,136, and the decrease of paper currency, exclusive of silver certificates, $30,388,289. In the foregoing tables the silver certificates issued by the Treasury have not been included, but the standard silver dollars held for the redemption on presentation form a portion of the silver coin in the Treasury. The silver certificates in the hands of the people and the banks at the following dates, were as follows:—

January 1, 1879	$413,360
November 1, 1880	19,780,240
November 1, 1881	58,838,770
November 1, 1882	65,620,450
November 1, 1883	85,334,381
November 1, 1884	100,741,562

It will be seen that the amount of these certificates in circulation has increased $15,407,180 during the year 1884.

The gold certificates issued under Section 12 of the Act of July 12, 1882, outstanding in the hands of the people and banks on November 1, 1882, November 1, 1883, and November 1, 1884, not including the amount in the Treasury, were $6,962,280, $48,869,040, and $85,301,190, respectively.

As before stated, the total amount of standard silver dollars coined up to November 1, 1884, was $184,730,829, of which, as shown in one of the foregoing tables, $142,926,726 was then in the Treasury, although an amount equal to $100,741,561 was represented by certificates in the hands of the people and the banks, leaving 42,185,165 then held by the Treasury. Of the $184,730,829 coined, $41,804,103 was, therefore, evidently outside of the Treasury, and $100,741,561 of the amount in the Treasury was represented by certificates in circulation. The remainder of the silver, $91,004,610, consisted of subsidiary coin, trade dollars, and bullion purchased for coinage, of which $33,993,284 was in the Treasury, and about $57,011,326 was in use with the people and the banks, consisting principally of subsidiary coin, in the place of the paper fractional currency for which it was substituted.

The increase of gold and silver coin and paper currency, exclusive of silver certificates, outside of the Treasury and the banks, since the date of resumption, is thus estimated to have been $263,956,936, and the decrease during the year ending November 1, 1883, $6,306,372. To these sums the amounts of silver certificates in the hands of the people may be added. On November 1, 1883, the amount of these certificates held by the people and the banks was, as has been seen, $100,741,561 ; but the proportion of this amount in the hands of the people cannot be exactly determined.

THE CITY OF WASHINGTON.

Is situated at the head of the navigable
waters of the Potomac River, as beautiful
a sheet of water as ever drained a valley,
and in a line nearly south of the Executive
Mansion. It takes a broad sweep to the
left when looking northward from the Ar-
senal, where it divides and forms what is
known as the Eastern Branch; this turns to
the right, and forms a channel to the Navy
Yard, thence northward into the northern
part of Maryland, while the river proper
turns to the left and passes West Washington and Georgetown to the Great Falls.
The water is generally clear above the
Falls, and furnishes the Washingtonians
plenty of excellent drinking water. When
the improved waterworks are completed,
the people of Washington will realize its
benefits for centuries to come.

Washington is mostly on high ground,
and the health of the city is excellent. It

has been said there is some malaria, but
that may be affirmed of almost any locality.
When the great improvements are completed on the flats, this will be obviated.
The climate surpasses that of most other
cities, for it is almost free from severe gales,
and the mercury does not change so rapidly
as at other places. The salt atmosphere
coming from the Chesapeake Bay, across
the western neck of Maryland, is purified
by passing through the forests before it
reaches the District of Columbia.

The private residences are some of the
finest in the world; and many have built
what are termed winter residences. In a
short time Washington will be known as
a winter resort for the best society in the
country, as it has the different representatives of every nation, and its own representatives from every congressional district.
It is a city composed of persons who, in the
course of events, or for want of employment,
have come here and settled. There are
at least 10,500 Government employees in
the District of Columbia, a great number

of whom are experts in their business,
strictly honest, to my personal knowledge;
and in the many years that they have been
employed, have laid up sufficient funds to
buy themselves homes. There are also
those who have not taken the precaution to
save for "a wet day," but have spent their
salary as soon as earned. A great number
of ladies are employed, who would, in the
event of removal, be turned out of house
and home. I heard a very strong Democratic lady, who has no personal interest in
the departments, a resident of the City of
Alexandria, Va., make the remark, that
she prayed God they might be spared, if
possible, from removal. They should have
the sympathy of every American citizen, for
they are highly educated, refined and respectable, and move in the best circles of
society.

The business of the city is conducted as
in all other large cities: it has some manufacturing interests, but is not what is termed
a manufacturing city.

Its inhabitants are composed mostly of

business men, who are engaged in the mercantile and commission business, and many live here who have business in all parts of the United States.

All kinds of stock are sold on exchange here, as in New York; mining stock in silver, gold, iron, lead, copper, coal and isinglass, railroad stock and grain exchange. Insurance companies, both for fire and life, have main and branch offices in Washington.

The increase of its population stimulates building, and houses of different modern styles are extensively built and readily sold or rented. A large amount of real estate has changed hands at advanced prices, and property is eagerly bought, if in a good locality.

The City of Washington will, in a short time, stand out like some great master-piece of art. It has been called the " Paris of America." Be that as it may, to-day it is a cleaner, more respectable and beautiful city, and is preferable to Paris with its grandeur and vices.

Its streets are the finest in the world, being perfectly smooth and clean. They are swept by machines, both day and night. The Avenue, which is the great thoroughfare of the city, can only be cleaned at night.

The public grounds and parks of this city are among its most attractive features. They are carefully kept ; the trees are always in perfect trim, the grass free from every twig or leaf that the restless wind might scatter upon its green, velvety surface. In these parks will be seen the statues of our noted heroes, of land and water, who have immortalized their names in immortalizing their country.

Its churches are among the finest in the nation. Here all denominations are represented, and a very good example of Christian spirit is manifested, as there does not appear to be any strife between the different churches or sects, as occurs so often in other cities, and a great detriment to the cause of Christianity.

The colored population of Washington is improving very fast in its habits and appearance. The greater part of them dress very respectably, and are a church-going people. They have numerous churches of modern style and accommodations, and are advancing fast in education and refinement. A great number of them are polite, obliging and respectable, and if encouraged, will soon make good citizens; the best way to do this is to set them good examples, and teach them to understand that if they ever wish to be respected, they must first learn to respect themselves, and act accordingly.

I can assure the colored people of America that in the next administration their rights will be acknowledged, the same as in the past, for in the President-elect they will find a man who is expected to, and who will protect his subjects, regardless of party, creed or color, provided they will first respect themselves.

THE PUBLIC BUILDINGS OF WASHINGTON.

The Executive Mansion, more popularly known as the White House, stands one mile west of the Capitol. It faces to the north, on Pennsylvania Avenue, and with its grounds occupying the whole block between Sixteenth and Seventeenth streets.

It is built of sandstone, painted white, hence the name, "White House." This building is of fine architecture, considering the time in which it was built.

It contains thirty-four rooms, all of which are very elaborately furnished. The upper story is occupied by the family, while the ground floor is devoted to reception rooms. The conservatory attached contains plants of many rare species, whose fragrant odors perfume these spacious halls.

The grounds of this mansion are very extensive, and are ornamented with fine shade trees and shubbery ; the lawns are

127

beautifully kept, and comprise about seventy-five acres.

The Capitol.   This building has no equal. It is built of white marble, and combines utility, beauty and strength.   There is no other building on the continent so stately, majestic and awe-inspiring.   It alone will richly repay any pleasure seeker for a careful examination and study, as the different designs, sculpture and pictures are among the finest in the world.   It stands on a hill, called "Capitol Hill," covering nearly four acres of ground, and overlooks the greater part of the city.

Its grounds will compare with any in Europe, the walks and drives being kept perfectly clean and neat.

This magnificent building is mostly constructed of white marble; its length is 750 feet, its greatest width, 325 feet; its height to the top of the dome, 229 feet.

The dome is of iron and surmounted by a bronze statue of the Goddess of Liberty, which was placed in position December 3, 1863; her height is nineteen feet and weight 14,880 pounds (rather tall and heavy for a miss in her teens).

The two largest chambers in the Capitol are situated—the one, the House of Representatives, in the south, the other, the Senate Chamber, in the north.

Congress begins its yearly session in these at twelve o'clock on the first Monday in December; and during the hours that it is in session, the American colors float in the breeze over each chamber. The present cost of the building, inclusive of grounds, is about $17,000,000, and its value to the nation is double that amount.

The War, State and Navy Departments are situated on the south side of Pennsylvania Avenue, between Seventeenth and Eighteenth streets. This magnificent building has not yet been completed, but when completed will rank among the finest in the world. It has all the improvements which money, time and ingenuity could suggest, and is perfect in its architecture. It contains 327 rooms, exclusive of the halls.

The United States Treasury. This

I

building is situated one mile to the west of the Capitol, on Fifteenth Street and Pennsylvania Avenue. It is a very massive structure, and covers nearly two acres. It is a piece of great architectural grandeur, substantially built, and will last until the end of time. Its vaults are filled with gold and silver. It is six stories high, its length 509 feet, and contains 400 rooms.

The building is not very well ventilated, and the employees have a tendency to look delicate, as the confinement is very great ; but when vacation is allowed them they improve quickly, and in thirty days, which is the extent of their vacation, they return very much benefited.

The Patent office is situated directly north of the Post Office. This building occupies two squares between F and G, and Seventh and Ninth streets, N. W. It is built of white marble, fronting on F street, but has entrances on G, Seventh and Ninth streets. It is three stories high, and contains 205 rooms, exclusive of halls and galleries, where models of patents are exhibited. It was partly destroyed by fire in 1876, but is now restored and in much better condition than ever before. This department is self-sustaining, and has upward of $2,000,000 at its credit in the Treasury.

There are a large number of employees in this Department who are engaged in examining patents, which are on the increase, and in some branches the examiners are months behind time, and unless the force is increased they will be unable to complete the work, which is accumulating daily.

The Post Office Department, which is situated between E and F, and Seventh and Eighth streets, N. W., occupying the entire square, is built of white marble, and is very massive. It is three stories high, and contains 255 rooms exclusive of halls. It has a branch on the west side of Eighth street, connected to the Post Office proper by a bridge over the street. This branch of the Department is built of brick.

Pension Office. This building, which is in course of construction, is situated in Judiciary Square, and is mostly built of brick, beautifully designed. The ceilings are all

arch-work and fire-proof. It will be completed in the early part of 1885, and when
finished, it will contain 90 rooms, exclusive
of halls.

It is a master-piece of art, and the venti-
lation is supposed to be perfect. It will
take many millions of bricks to complete this
structure. Congress made an appropriation for its erection.

The National Museum. This fine structure stands on the Smithsonian grounds,
just east of Smithsonian Institute, and
covers upwards of two acres.

It is a new building; was only completed
in 1882. It is constructed of brick, and
cost about $251,000; its dome is ninety-two
feet above the surface of the ground. It
contains many curiosities from different
nations.

Adjacent to this building is the Smithsonian
Institute, filled with anthropological curiosities, and mineralogical and zoölogical col-
lections, nearly all of which were bequeathed
to the people of the United States by an
English gentleman, by the name of James
Smithson, for the benefit of science.

WASHINGTON MONUMENT.

This great work of art in masonry is one of the highest in the world, its height being 555 feet, and the smallest stone in it weighs more than two tons. It was commenced in the year 1842, and after it had attained the height of 215 feet the work was stopped, on account of the lack of funds, which were raised by contribution, but later on Congress appropriated sufficient funds to complete it.

After a careful examination, it was decided that the old foundation was insufficient to support the structure.

It was, therefore, decided to put in a new one, which was done by running drifts underneath the monument, filled with concrete, made of the best cement, broken stone and gravel.

This was so carefully done that at no time was the obelisk more than one-fourth of an inch out of plumb. And now, at the height of 555 feet, it is not one-eighth of an inch out of a perpendicular line.

It is capped with a pyramid of aluminium, nine inches high and five inches square at its base, which serves as a lightning conductor and is connected by a rod through the top stone with a well below the foundation. This is said to form one of the most complete arrangements known for the conduction of electricity.

The monument stands on public grounds, nearly south of the Executive Mansion, and in a direct line with the Potomac river, and looking from a point two miles down the river it appears in its full beauty.

The report of the Monument Commission shows that the weight of the monument is 81,120 tons, and that it has cost $1,187,710, of which Congress appropriated $887,710. Relative to the completion of the monument, the engineer in charge of the work submits a report with that of the Commission. He says:—

"Two methods of treating the terrace at the foot of the shaft have been suggested— one proposing to erect a retaining wall, of the most beautiful marble, around the terrace, which wall is to be surmounted with a marble balustrade. At the centre of each face is to be a set of broad, double stairs, extending from the general level of the esplanade, which is to be paved in marble tiles of approved patterns. The other method of finish proposed is to fill earth about the present terrace, and to extend this filling so far from the monument as to blend the slopes of the embankment gradually into the surrounding surfaces ; and this is to be done with so much skill as to give to the mound an appearance as far from artificial as possible. This mound is then to be planted with trees and shrubs, and paths to be laid out. A pavement is to be put around the foot of the monument, extending far enough to prevent the storm-waters from washing out the filling."

If the marble wall is decided upon, an appropriation of $612,300 is asked, to complete the entire work. If the second proposition is adopted but $166,800 is desired. The joint Commission favor the latter method.

OUR COUNTRY.

The Northwestern States may boast of grain,
The Southern ones of wood and cane,
The Pacific slope of grapes and gold,
The Eastern ones of bitter cold.

Wisconsin of its lead and copper,
Minnesota of its large grain hopper,
Vermont of its mountains of evergreens,
Ohio and Illinois of their oats, pork and beans.

Virginia, Pennsylvania, of their iron, oil and lime,
Alabama, Florida, of oranges and sunny Winter
    clime,
Idaho and Nevado of their silver ores,
Kentucky of its horses and hospitable doors.

New York, Connecticut, the richest of the common-
    wealth,
Of their free institutions, and lasses of beauty and
    health;
They are more to them than iron, coal or grain,
With their cunning hand and cultured brain.

" For well they keep their ancient stock,
The stubborn strength of the Plymouth Rock ; "
Far better to them than copper or lead,
Are their fine young men with a level head.

"Nor heed they the bigot or skeptic hands,
While near the school the church spire stands;"
Nor fear they the old fogy rule,
While near the spire stands the school.

But suppose that bigots' and skeptics' tools
Should get control of our public schools—
The grass would grow where the college stands,
And our youths would be bound with iron bands;
And our advanced institutions, which stand out so
    free
In the language of Burns, will have " gang aglee."

Then let America's free sons all watch and beware,
Either Democrat or Republican, I do not care,
They both are interested in the welfare of state,—
If such foes should rise we must seal their fate.

So let men of foreign and skeptic principles know
That they must not come to the States to grow;
We will drive them back at the point of steel,
And let them our just indignation feel.

Then stand by the altars of your sires,
And maintain your rights and pure desires,
And while you watch around your little family band,
Remember God and your native land!

THE POTOMAC RIVER.

This beautiful sheet of water forms a dividing line between Virginia and Maryland, and it is one hundred miles in length from the Great Falls to Chesapeake Bay. It is noted for its great fisheries and game; thousands of ducks, geese and swan are constantly on its bosom, from the first of November until the latter part of March, when they take their flight northward. It very seldom freezes at its mouth, but in the upper waters, where it is fresh, ice sometimes forms to such an extent as to impede navigation.

There are many steamers plying between Norfolk, Philadelphia, New York and Baltimore; also a great many vessels, a large number of which are engaged in the oyster trade.

The farms along the river are generally well located; there are some bluffs along its shores, but mostly table land; its soil is inclined to be light, and is largely cultivated; corn, wheat and tobacco are raised. The land is cheap, and there are a number of farms for sale which would make nice homes near to Washington, where their products would find a good market.

Alexandria is the only town on its banks below Washington, with a water front sufficiently deep for the largest vessels to land. It has not grown much since the war, but in the last few years new enterprises have sprung up that promise to help it greatly. Its population is about 18,000. It is a good grain market, and supports a large number of commission men. It also has numerous stores of all kinds. Its inhabitants are of the first people of the commonwealth of Virginia.

THE HOME AND TOMB OF WASHINGTON.

Mount Vernon is seventeen miles down the river, and is situated directly on its bank, commanding a beautiful view to the east. The grounds and building are kept in good condition by a " Board of Regents."

Everything is done for the comfort of its visitors. The steamer Corcoran runs there daily, making the trip in two hours, and at the low rate of one dollar for the round trip. Captain Blake, a very popular man, sees to the comfort of his passengers, and visitors always return very much pleased. The steamer starts from Seventh Street wharf, at 9 A. M., returning at 3 P. M., thus allowing two hours at the tomb of Washington. One can always enjoy a very pleasant time on this trip.

SUMMER RESORTS.

The only accessible resort Washington has is a new place called "Colonial Beach," a beautiful shore on the Potomac, sixty miles from Washington. The river is very wide here and forms a bay, which is twelve miles one way and eight the other. The shore is perfect and lovely; three-fourths of the year one can spend there as a summer resort, enjoying the luxuries of salt water, in game, fish, oysters, crabs, and also delicious berries, which grow wild in all the

fields ; dew, black, huckle and straw-
berries too, when cultivated, grow luxuri-
antly. The bathing cannot be surpassed,
and from the first of June until October the
water is sufficiently warm. It is noted for its
springs, which supply good drinking water.
There is one thing very peculiar, that is,
those that go there are always benefited,
they get an appetite at once, and the salt air
also seems to help their digestive organs.
There is a very nice hotel, newly built,
which, after this season, is intended to be
kept open the entire year.

It has been surveyed in lots, and upwards
of five hundred have been sold. They are
50 x 150 feet, and quite a number of their
owners have built very comfortable cottages
on them. The place has the appearance of
a rising western town ; all this has been
done within the last two years, and it prom-
ises to become a popular resort for Washington and its surrounding country.

There are no mosquitoes to bother the
weary, and it is perfectly healthy. All will
find it a delightful place to spend their sum-

mer vacation, in a profitable and enjoyable manner.

The steamers Arrowsmith, J. W. Thompson and Mattane, which ply down the river, stop there, and the fare is very cheap, less than one cent per mile. These boats leave every day, at 7 A. M., from Seventh Street wharf, and reach the beach at 1 P. M.; returning next day, leaving the beach at 8 A. M. and arriving at Washington about 3 P. M.

Next season there will be a boat to make special round trips daily, to the beach, to accommodate its patrons.

There will also be another, which is now being built by the Washington Steamboat Company Limited, which will ply on the Potomac, and which will be a model of beauty, swiftness and comfort.

A trip down this river is ever enjoyable, as the Potomac is one of the prettiest of rivers, and the scenery along its banks of evergreens is picturesque in the extreme.

GROWING EVILS OF OUR COUNTRY.

A habit of the greater part of our young men is seemingly destined to bring them into trouble, as it seems, a singular idea has come into their heads that every young man must carry in his hip-pocket a revolver, and on the least pretext the hip-pocket is resorted to at once. Unless something is done to stop such cowardice there is no telling when a man's life is in safety.

There is in almost every daily paper an account of the accidental shooting of some person by the careless handling of a pistol. That there should be some rigid law by which such persons should be punished, is manifest.

The colored population is fast falling into the same habit, of not only carrying, but using them with impunity.

This using of firearms in large cities should be stopped at once, and if Congress does not pass a strict law, that will be enforced with effect, no one knows what the consequences may be. Suicide and murder are on the increase since this habit began, and if continued the crimes will be manifold.

When this nuisance is stopped it will make a great difference to all good citizens; the sooner it falls the better. Every city is interested in this evil, but in this District, Congress must provide for its speedy cure.

If national and citizen life is to be enjoyed by a nation and its people, it is necessary for both to endeavor to assist one another to obtain the greatest benefits therefrom, and to accomplish this, the great object of a nation should be to protect itself from wars, and from whatever goes to demoralize its people.

War always means destruction of body and property, and demoralization in many instances.

The method of deciding matters of importance and variances, should be left to arbitration—a subject that all nations should consider with the greatest amount of interest.

To settle a small matter there might be a woful destruction of life and property; and then does the nation in the right always get justice? or in other words, does might make right? No man will answer yes, for brutal or other force may capture the innocent, but how long can it keep them? Only as long as it keeps them bound.

The true way to settle national difficulties is by a council of arbitration, and if all nationalists would agree to this its judgment could always be enforced, as all nations would at once hold the responsible party to account.

This subject is being now agitated by our best citizens of the Church of Brotherly Love, the Quakers; and all true Christians will agree to the doctrines of a peace conference on the basis of right and wrong, and on that decision let the one in the wrong pay the utmost farthing.

This method will apply also to individuals, and, if properly considered, will save much time and expense in long litigation and bad feelings, which always exist after such litigation.

Arbitration generally ends in making the contestants friends, instead of enemies.

The Arbitration League is an organization which is a step in the right direction to save blood and devastation, and will bring forth fruit of peace and love toward God and man.

But our nation seems more like an individual, as she is governed by the people, and the dangers are the same identically. For there is more danger from our inside foes than from our outside enemies.

Therefore, this nation should at all times have no less than 50,000 men employed as a standing army. There is no better way of judging of the future than by reflecting on the past.

Look back at our Rebellion; and look at the great strikes of 1877 at Pittsburgh; and again at the recent riot at Cincinnati. We have a peculiar people, and there is need of our country being watched; and, as I have stated before in this book, if this country was worth our forefathers' blood and time to gain it, it certainly should be our desire to protect it at all times, lest, when we think not, we may be in the midst of foes.

This is a subject that should interest every Christian citizen, and likewise all law-abiding men.

Another evil Congress ought to act upon at once is the tramp nuisance. This country is overrun with a great many poor, worthless vagrants, upon which Congress should pass an act that all the States could ratify.

The thefts, arsons and outrages committed by the tramps are almost every day chronicled in the press. It is high time to stop such crime.

Congress should pass a law that would give any constable, policeman, or marshal the power to arrest such vagrants, take them before a United States marshal, try them, and if found guilty take them at once and press them into the United States military service for five years.

But says one, the taxes are too heavy now, and that would add a larger expense to our country.

As it is the taxes are large, and are paid by a few around the outskirts of the cities and rural districts, and they pay taxes to support the tramps, but at a fearful cost: barns burned, thefts, and the worst of all crimes, outrage.

This pressing them into the service would go a great way toward helping these poor beings to become of some value to themselves and the Government. If, on examination, they should be found unfit for service, send them to the workhouse, and keep them for not less than three years.

This law should also provide for criminals to reclaim themselves by giving them the privilege to enlist in the army after one-third of their time is served. For instance, if a man was sent to the State prison for five years, he should, after the expiration of two years, have the right to enlist for five years in the service, which would discipline him, and at the end of that time get an honor-

able discharge, to show when in want of
work. Now, a criminal, after having served
out his time, is at once turned out with a
small amount of money, which will be unable to sustain him more than a few days,
and if in want of work will have to tell a lie
or not get employment, for it is customary
to ask where they have been previously
employed.

It would be well for Congress to consider
this subject.

THE DEFEATED CANDIDATES.

JAMES G. BLAINE, the defeated candidate, is one of the smartest political men that America has ever produced, and had it not been for his vanity, he would not have made the great mistake which he did when he advised Garfield to appoint Robinson to the office of Collector of the Port of New York, without any consultation with Conkling. But Blaine, like other men, saw his mistake after it was made. The supporters of Blaine made a noble stand, and James G. can only thank Blaine for his defeat. Of course, he could not expect support from his enemies; therefore he cannot blame them.

JOHN A. LOGAN deserves the sympathy of the American people, and I trust he will have it, not alone from the men, but from the boys; for in his simple allusion to his misfortune, he stated, it is said, that he was like a boy that stubbed his toe; it hurt too much to laugh and he was too big to cry. In this we see a true man, and the American nation will remember him for it; and I hope at some future day he will receive their support.

PLYMOUTH ROCK.

THE AMERICAN EAGLE.

When the Pilgrims on Plymouth Rock did land,
Liberty on this continent did first make her stand,
And a few people, in a forest wild,
Gave thanks to God, and He in answer smiled.

Although few in number was that little flock,
Yet millions now give thanks in memory of the Ply-
	mouth Rock;
The eagle, perched on the gigantic oak,
Watched with an acute eye the axman's stroke:
The Pilgrim did return that gaze,
On that wondrous bird of liberty amazed;
Not alone did this sight occupy his mind;
It seemed to be an omen of the liberty he wished to
	find,
The long sought home of the Christian's aspiration;
And he thought of the tyrant's kingdom with indig-
	nation;
And when the eagle left that oak to soar on high,
He resolved to live for liberty, if necessary for her to
	die.

And as the monarch of the sky made his circuit through
	vast space,
In this little band of Pilgrims the thoughts of liberty
	kept pace;

On they struggled, until 1776, the 4th of July,
When once more they made the declaration for lib-
    erty to live, for her to die.

Then in solemn thanks their Preserver they praised;
And as an emblem of liberty on their standard raised
The American eagle, so fierce and so bold,
In polished brass, or glittering gold,
An emblem of freedom, swiftness and power,
Which they felt they would need in the coming hour.

Then fiercely growled the British lion,
To think of the growth of the Pilgrims' scion,
And England filled her guns with iron hail;
But to no purpose; our braves did not quail;
And she poured her shot on Bunker Hill;
But as the sun rose next morn, their flag was there
    still,
And the American eagle perched on its top, ever bold,
While many a British lay stiff and cold,
Where their comrades had deserted them in their
    eager flight,
And left them to die in the cold, damp night.

The Revolution had begun, and the blow had told
That the sons of the Pilgrims were both fierce and
    bold;
Which they ever have shown in their defensive
    fights,
And have ever been victorious in their just principles
    and rights.

The God of Hosts has ever been their guide ;
And now they have millions of brothers to stand by
    their side ;
And for the American Eagle, in war or in peace,
As an emblem of freedom, our love will ne'er cease !